TEMPTING DEATH
ON A TEST-FLIGHT TO
THE UNKNOWN

The take off was perfectly normal, and Spate's rocket fighter was soon streaking up into the sky. It disappeared from view, and then we spotted his contrail. Soon he was plummeting down like a meteor and we held our breath. He touched down perfectly but now on the frozen grass he was skidding across the field at tremendous speed. The aircraft gave no sign of slowing down and was rapidly approaching the perimeter. Then, something totally unexpected happened. The cockpit canopy flew off and Spate's body whirled through the air, striking the wing and then bouncing on the ground, the fighter careering on at more than a hundred kilometers per hour! I noticed a mechanic beside me make the sign of the cross and, metaphorically, I did also. At that moment the runaway aircraft turned over on its back and disappeared in a brilliant flash, debris being thrown in every direction.

THE BANTAM WAR BOOK SERIES

This series of books is about a world on fire.

The carefully chosen volumes in the Bantam War Book Series cover the full dramatic sweep of World War II. Many are eyewitness accounts by the men who fought in a global conflict as the world's future hung in the balance. Fighter pilots, tank commanders and infantry captains, among many others, recount exploits of individual courage. They present vivid portraits of brave men, true stories of gallantry, moving sagas of survival and stark tragedies of untimely death.

In 1933 Nazi Germany marched to become an empire that was to last a thousand years. In only twelve years that empire was destroyed, and ever since, the country has been bisected by her conquerors. Italy relinquished her colonial lands, as did Japan. These were the losers. The winners also lost the empires they had so painfully seized over the centuries. And one, Russia, lost over twenty million dead.

Those wartime 1940s were a simple, even a hopeful time. Hats came in only two colors, white and black, and after an initial battering the Allied nations started on a long and laborious march toward victory. It was a time when sane men believed the world would evolve into a decent place, but, as with all futures, there was no one then who could really forecast the world that we know now.

There are many ways to think about that war. It has always been hard to understand the motivations and braveries of Axis soldiers fighting to enslave and dominate their neighbors. Yet it is impossible to know the hammer without the anvil, and to comprehend ourselves we must know the people we once fought against.

Through these books we can discover what it was like to take part in the war that was a final experience for nearly fifty million human beings. In so doing we may discover the strength to make a world as good as the one contained in those dreams and aspirations once believed by heroic men. We must understand our past as an honor to those dead who can no longer choose. They exchanged their lives in a hope for this future that we now inhabit. Though the fight took place many years ago, each of us remains as a living part of it.

ROCKET FIGHTER

Mano Ziegler
Translated by Alexander Vanags

**With a Foreword
by Lieut.-Gen. Adolf Galland (Rtd.)**

BANTAM BOOKS
TORONTO • NEW YORK • LONDON • SYDNEY • AUCKLAND

This low-priced Bantam Book
has been completely reset in a type face
designed for easy reading, and was printed
from new plates. It contains the complete
text of the original hard-cover edition.
NOT ONE WORD HAS BEEN OMITTED.

ROCKET FIGHTER

A Bantam Book / published by arrangement with
Doubleday & Company, Inc.

PRINTING HISTORY

First published in the German language in 1961 as
Raketenjager Me 163 by Motor-Presse-Verlag, Gmbh, Stuttgart.
This translation © Macdonald & Co. (Publishers) Ltd., 1963
Doubleday edition published October 1963

Bantam edition / July 1984

Cover art by Bill Phillips, whose paintings are on display
at The National Air & Space Museum in Washington, D.C.

Maps by Alan McKnight.
Illustration by Greg Beecham and Tom Beecham.

ISBN 0-553-24179-6

Published simultaneously in the United States and Canada

PRINTED IN THE UNITED STATES OF AMERICA

O   0 9 8 7 6 5 4 3 2 1

To Our Unforgettable Heini Dittmar

Kiel

BALTIC SEA

Peenemünde

Hamburg

Rechlin

Lüneburg
Heath

Stendal

Berlin

Hanover
Brunswick
Brandenburg
Templehof Kreuzberg

Magdeburg

Dessau

SAXONY

Halle
Mokkau
Zeidlitza Brandis
Leipzig

R M A N Y

Wasserkuppe
ohe Rhön

NORTHWESTERN
GERMANY

Miles
0 10 20   40   60

Kilometers
0   20 40 60 80 100

Foreword

by
LIEUTENANT-GENERAL ADOLF GALLAND (RTD.)

THE FIGHTER AIRCRAFT whose story is told in this book signified a technical sensation in aerial warfare when it first became operational in our Home Air Defence. It was the world's first manned rocket-powered aircraft and, as such, it was perhaps a decade ahead of its time.

When the Me 163 came under my command for operational tests, it was still technically immature and was not available in sufficient numbers to be a decisive weapon. To fly this aircraft was still a gamble between life and death. Some thirty men had volunteered to flight-test this novel machine, and only they—and the genial designers Lippisch, Walter, Messerschmitt and a few others—knew its secrets.

This book rescues from oblivion the story of the dramatic events that led to the Me 163s eventual introduction on operations, and its first operational sorties. Accordingly, I wish this book—whose author himself took part as a pilot in the flight-testing of this historic aircraft—every success, serving as it will as a tribute to those brave men who gave their lives to bring this revolutionary development to maturity.

Author's Preface

THIS IS NOT REALLY A WAR STORY, although its events took place during the Second World War; it is the story of an aircraft and the men who flew it. The Messerschmitt 163, designed by Alexander Lippisch, was the world's first controllable rocket-powered aircraft, and the men who flew it were the world's first rocket pilots. It was the first aircraft in the world to exceed a thousand kilometres per hour in level flight, and it came closer to touching the sound barrier than any other aircraft of its time.

In many respects the Me 163 was a pioneer; it was certainly one of the most remarkable aircraft in the history of military aviation. It was some ten years ahead of its time, but the stress of war accelerated its development and, because of that, it was also probably the most dangerous aircraft ever to be built in series. When it was first created and flown, few knew of its existence. All files in which reference was made to this aircraft were stamped "Most Secret", and all concerned with it were sworn to absolute secrecy—secrecy that was maintained until the last day of the war.

With the end of the war, the men who had accompanied the Me 163 on its way and who were still alive—the designers, technicians and pilots—were scattered throughout the world, as were also most of the records, reports and photographs which told the story of this amazing machine. Little remained to be salvaged.

And so this book came into being—compiled from memory, from diaries, and from talks with those concerned with this aircraft and who survived. I have endeavoured to present to you, the reader, an accurate and truthful report of the events of those hectic days. My own experiences and sentiments undoubtedly colour this account, but it contains no fiction. To me, it has not seemed so important to list dates and assemble data as to tell the human side of this story and to record our flying experiences which were, in many ways, unique. Above all, it has seemed important to leave a story to posterity of a group of pilots who gave themselves freely to a task of flight-testing fraught with more dangers than any before; a task which lasted for twenty long months and during which they daily walked a tightrope between life and death.

Most of them lost their lives, but their lives had not been wasted, for those experiences which, at the time had demanded so many sacrifices, were to help other pilots in other countries as they pressed nearer toward the sound barrier armed with the knowledge gained from work carried out by Test-Commando 16.

Mano Ziegler

Contents

1

Test-Commando 16

IT WAS a delightful July day in 1943 when I climbed from that antiquated little train in Bad Zwischenahn, Oldenburg, leaving it to roll its ancient wheels "for victory" in pathetic simplicity. I glanced up at a cloudless blue sky; a sky that for some time past had hidden a secret which had made its whispered rounds among fighter pilots. A manned rocket aircraft—terribly fast—climbing like an arrow! Impossible. Such a contraption could not possibly exist. It was too absurd . . . yet, was it? I stood on the platform of the little railway station, peering curiously into an empty sky. But was it empty? As I watched, a tiny black speck appeared, growing with phenomenal speed into a boomerang-shaped object which turned, dived, levelled-off, and swept past as soundless as a phantom, and then, confound it, disappeared behind the trees.

The guard at the entrance of the airfield could not have viewed me with more suspicion had I been wearing a pair of swimming trunks and a wig. He carefully examined my posting orders, apparently unable to believe that a certain Lieutenant Ziegler had been ordered to report to Test-Commando 16 at Bad Zwischenahn, but my paybook confirmed the fact that I was the aforesaid Lieutenant, and finally he allowed me to pass into a world which, officially, did not even exist, the Nirvana of GeKados*. Suddenly I was startled by an ear-splitting roar. It sounded as though an immense red hot iron had been plunged into a huge bathtub—a veritable hiss of Siegfried's dragon! My head spun around and my surprised eyes saw a violet-black cloud driving a leaping, skipping "something" ahead of it, faster and faster until the object leaped from the ground, jettisoned a pair of wheels, and shot up into the sky. By the time I had closed my mouth, which had opened in astonishment, the thing has disappeared. There was nothing left to indicate that I had not suffered an hallucination apart from a dissolving violet-grey smoke trail. A little while later the strange craft reappeared and, like the other I had seen when standing on the station platform, glided soundlessly through the air, circled, and dropped on to the ground.

I could not restrain my curiosity, and ran towards the spot where the thing now lay like a tired butterfly. And so we became acquainted, the "Powered Egg" and I, and one by one I met the others who, pilots from various German fighter units, barely thirty in number, had come as volunteers or had been ordered to Bad Zwischenahn to lead a new wonder weapon towards its baptism of fire.

Later that first afternoon I discovered that the smoking and hissing thing, with which I had made fleeting acquaintance earlier, was not the true "Powered Egg" at all, but only its forerunner, the Messerschmitt Me 163A, a few examples of which had been built solely to familiarize us with the peculiarities of rocket-powered flight. "To trust is to honour," I thought, as I accompanied Otto Oertzen and Herbert Langer to the big hangar in which I could examine the little monster at my leisure, and have its idiosyncrasies explained to me. Otto was one of our engineers, and Herbert, a very young First Lieutenant, was aide-de-camp to our com-

---

*An abbreviation of Geheime Kommandosache (Secret Command), a unit whose activities demanded the greatest possible secrecy.

manding officer who, it appeared, was absent at that time. And there she was, squatting in the twilight of the hanger, as graceful as a young bat—the Me 163A. Otto opened a hatch in the fuselage and I peered at the maze of pipes which resembled nothing more than the innards of a refrigerator. This, they said, was the engine! Through one of these pipes flowed Z-stoff and through another T-stoff, the two being sprayed into the combustion chamber where they immediately ignited to develop a thrust equivalent to some two thousand horsepower. Otto and Herbert kept on talking, like two professors of zoology lecturing on the bone structure of an Ichthyosaurus, a subject with which I should have been equally conversant, for not being an engineering type, their discourse passed way above my head. Only the reference to a thrust equivalent to some two thousand horsepower made any impression on me. This was a tangible figure if, at the same time, an inconceivable one in view of the small size of the rocket motor. Two thousand horsepower to propel one member of the genus homo through the air—yes, indeed, this was impressive!

My next strange discovery was made, of all places, in the mess. Items that had long since been promoted to precious festive menus were to be had here as a matter of course at every meal, every day! Creamed rice with fruit preserves, delicious omelettes with kidneys, blossom-white macaroni with goulash, and countless other dishes that had long ago disappeared from German tables. And for breakfast? Poached or scrambled eggs on toast; toast made with real *white* bread! Black bread was simply unheard of here, and such repasts were accompanied by *real* tea and coffee. When I enquired the reason for such superb food I heard for the first time the ominous term "altitude diet". Staff Physician Doctor Dunker, a specialist in high-altitude flying problems who had been specially transferred to our unit, explained to me that the Me 163 operated at altitudes the effects of which on the human body were still very much like a closed book, as were also those resulting from the tremendous climbing and diving speeds of the rocket fighter. In fact, the so-called "altitude diet" was nothing more than a preventive measure designed to avoid indigestible or flatulence-causing foods, which we would have regretted having eaten when we attained the higher altitudes. I sadly bade farewell, therefore, to my favourite dish—pea soup with bacon! The doctor mentioned in passing that he was expecting to see me the very next morning in the low-pressure chamber for my first high-altitude aptitude test!

I had still to report to the commanding officer who arrived later that evening in his Messerschmitt Taifun, but, in all honesty, I harboured more than a little apprehensiveness regarding this interview. My request to be transferred to rocket aircraft had been refused on two previous occasions because, they said, I was "too old". Indeed, with all my thirty-five years, I was considered an "old man" by *normal* fighter-pilot standards, and to these rocket specialists I was Methuselah himself! But I was soon to discover that I had little need to be apprehensive, for Wolfgang Späte, our commanding officer who had nearly a hundred victories to his credit and Oak Leaves to his Knight's Cross, proved very friendly. I was immediately attracted to Späte as a man,

Knight's Cross with Oak Leaves and Swords

and I even forgave him for the fact that he obviously did not expect too much of me in view of my antiquity. He was a fellow who would accept nothing less than a one hundred per cent effort as long as one was on duty, but off duty he was immediately one of the "bunch".

Our "bunch" was certainly an odd crowd, and reminded me of a pirate crew from the Middle Ages. Coming from practically every Fighter Geschwader of the Luftwaffe, and posted to Bad Zwischenahn from the Russian front, France, Africa, Italy or Finland, every man was an individualist, their characters differing one from another so widely that, notwithstanding their common language, the sparks were continually flying. But despite innumerable differences of opinion, we were a "bunch". Our life in the months ahead was often to be hard, but this only welded us together more closely until we were to be as one in comradeship, duty and willingness.

It started the very next morning in the low-pressure chamber. This particular piece of equipment had been captured in the Soviet Union, and was a steel colossus half the size of a railway carriage. Dr. Dunker invited us to enter the chamber by means of a mighty steel door, reminiscent of that of a bank vault, and the interior proved to be rather like the crew room of a submarine. There was a long desk with pencils and paper, and I sat between Herbert Langer and Fritz Kelb, both of whom had arrived a few days earlier and were presumably already wise to this fun. The door clanged shut, and Dunker's magnified eyes could be seen observing our reactions through a "spy hole" in the upper part of the door. I hadn't had the dubious pleasure of a trip in a submarine, but what was to follow in this low-pressure chamber was probably much the same as in a submarine when the order to flood tanks is given. Fritz commented dryly that a few men had already died in this chamber. "And others froze to death," added Herbert as a hissing and gargling like a whole regiment of recruits at a tooth-cleaning parade began to fill the chamber, and a dial before my eyes climbed steadily to a thousand . . . two thousand . . . three thousand . . . four thousand metres. Simultaneously, the chamber grew colder and colder. We clutched pencils in our hands and began writing numerals on the paper in front of us: 1-2-3-4-5-6-7-8. . . ! When the dial was nearing the seven thousand metre mark I noticed that my right hand had begun to twitch but I continued writing. Next to me, Fritz started humming a tune, and I joined him, while Herbert was prattling away unintelligibly. The twitching in my right hand began to increase, and the pencil between my fingers began to behave like a blindworm robbed of its Sunday sleep. The needle in the dial quivered around the eight thousand metre mark. The noise level in the chamber dropped temporarily, and then, accompanied by a tremendous hissing, the needle in the dial began to swing backwards. Somewhere around four thousand metres Fritz became noticeably livelier while Herbert was kneading his fingers. I felt like a mole awakening from a long winter sleep, and I could not help chuckling at the strings of figures on the paper in front of me. The first lines stood there clean and neat, but gradually they became clumsy, looking as though they had been written by an octogenarian. My "plus six thousand metres" lines were pleated and they changed into a series of erratic hieroglyphs around the seven thousand metre mark!

When the air pressure between our steel box and the outside world had equalized, Dr. Dunker opened the door and I soon discovered some interesting facts about myself. Unbeknown to me I had nearly passed over permanently around the eight thousand metre mark. In fact, a few more minutes and Fritz, Herbert and I would have been walking hand in hand towards Valhalla. Had the good doctor delayed a while in turning that handwheel! There and then I decided to remain on the friendliest possible terms with the Herr Doctor, I was now informed that we had to undergo this ordeal every day in order to achieve the standard of fitness demanded by flight at extreme altitudes and, more important, to learn to recognize all symptoms of altitude sickness. The latter was of the utmost importance. It could happen that our oxygen system malfunctioned or received damage from enemy fire, and if we were unable to recognize altitude sickness symptoms immediately we would have virtually no chance of returning to earth alive. We were told that immediately we experienced such symptoms it was our duty to put the nose of the fighter down and dive for the safety of the four thousand metre line. This all applied, of course, to any aircraft flying at extreme altitudes, but a climb to altitude taking perhaps thirty minutes in an orthodox fighter was an affair of hardly more than a minute in a rocket-driven fighter. With a sinking feeling in the pit of my stomach, I made way for the next batch of pressure chamber guinea-pigs and, together with Fritz and Herbert, made my way to the stores to collect the "Powered Egg" pilot's outfit. This included all the usual accessories, such as fur-lined boots, flying helmet with built-in headphones, R/T connection leads, parachute pack, flying gloves, etcetera, but to this pile was added a combination smock manufactured of allegedly acid-proof material! Fritz commented, seeing the question that I was about to ask, "When the T-stoff flows into your pants instead of finding its way into the combustion chamber you burn up like a firework, and this will slow down the process!" "How come?" I asked. "Well, it sometimes happens that a feedline develops a leak or a fuel tank explodes!" he replied. I needed no further explanation!

2

Practical Training Begins

THE PRACTICAL SIDE of my training as a rocket fighter pilot began on the same day, and as is so often the case when learning to do something that is fraught with danger, it began quite innocuously; in this case with flights in gentle gliders. Initially, these gliders were well-known types such as the Grunau Baby and the Kranich, but we soon graduated to a series of Habicht gliders with progressively shorter wing spans. With the gradual reduction of the wing span the landing speed rose commensurately, and our so-called Stummel-Habicht had the not inconsiderable landing speed of 62 m.p.h. which was quite something for a glider! Further along was to come the Me 163A which floated down at about 100 m.p.h., while the fully-equipped Me 163B Komet fighter touched down at 137 m.p.h.! To make matters still more interesting, such landings had to be accomplished without the aid of an orthodox undercarriage as the Komet jettisoned its wheels shortly after take-off, and a short, broad skid had to suffice to cushion the impact on touching down.

Accompanying the problem of such high-speed landings was the fact that the rocket pilot enjoyed no second chance if he muffed his first approach; he could not open up and go round again as could the pilot of an orthodox fighter. No matter from what altitude or direction he happened to be coming in, he had to calculate his gliding approach in such a way that he could touch down within a certain distance from the landing cross, leaving enough "sliding space" to decelerate from 137 m.p.h. to a standstill within the airfield. And so we began our training as "target-landing" specialists in harmless gliders.

Every pilot knows that learning to fly means little more than learning to land! While learning to land with the aid of his flying instructor he learns everything else more or less on the side. Flying a normal aeroplane on a fine day is easier than helping one's grandmother to wind her knitting wool, but when it comes to landing one has to be able to do the knitting oneself. Unfortunately, the Me 163 was a single-seater, and no amount of ingenuity on the part of the manufacturers could have found space in that tiny aircraft for a second seat. And so at Bad Zwischenahn we had to be *told* rather than shown how to land this incalculable little brute.

First and foremost, we had to remember to extend the flexible landing skid. To attempt a landing on a retracted skid was not only to invite damage to the aircraft; it would almost certainly ensure the dislocation of the pilot's spinal column! By and by I was to learn that flight trials with the Komet at Peenemünde had already taken their toll of vertebrae, and much more distinguished ones than mine at that. We were told that a dirty landing, or a landing outside the airfield perimeter, which would probably only bend an airscrew or crack a wing spar on an orthodox aircraft, could easily end in the Komet turning turtle with the result that the highly temperamental rocket fuels remaining in the tanks would explode, providing the pilot with quick oblivion. This danger of an explosion was not merely a possibility but highly probable in the event of a rough landing. Of course, I knew all about this so-called "anxiety talk" designed to deflate the ego of young joystick candidates, but this time even the superior feeling of being an old hand at the flying game offered me little comfort. I felt as naked and stupid as though I had turned up in the middle of a mess dance in my nightshirt. That combination of hydrogen-peroxide, hydrazine hydrate and methyl alcohol could provide both experienced and inexperienced, wary and unwary, with a surprise ticket to Valhalla.

I first began to experience this uncomfortable feeling of nakedness in our "poison kitchen"—the rocket engine hangar—when two of our engineers, Eli and Otto, first demonstrated for me the explosive power of the rocket fuels. Otto placed a saucer on the floor of the hangar and carefully poured in two or three thimbles full of white liquid. He then stood back and allowed a few droplets of another liquid to fall into the saucer. The results were instantaneous—a hiss, a bang, and a jet of flame all in one! Now, I am not easily startled, but when Eli remarked, "The Komet carries two tons of this stuff in its tanks!" the colour of my face must have paled perceptibly. Eli added that, in the case of the fuels of the Me 163A they were known as T-stoff and Z-stoff, whereas those of the Me 163B were T-stoff and C-stoff. The actual composition of the fuels hidden by those designations I discovered only much later—in fact, after the war. Such was the secrecy all around us at that time. Like babies, we didn't know what was being pushed into our mouths.

After this first demonstration, Otto bent over one of the buckets and dipped his forefinger in the liquid fuel. "Would you care to try it?" he asked. Just a quick dip and only to the first joint of my finger. I poked the tip of my finger into the liquid and withdrew it quickly. In a few seconds it turned white and began to burn! Otto already had his finger in his mouth and advised me laughingly to follow his example if I valued my finger. I wasted no time in putting my painful finger into my mouth, and almost immediately the saliva neutralized the effect of this devil's brew!

That evening I found myself alone. Fritz and Herbert were out on dates, the C.O. was away, and having nothing better to do, I decided to stroll into Bad Zwischenahn. A dignified old fellow, a combination of Bismarck and Wilhelm II, shared my table in a little restaurant, and, after a time, we struck up a conversation. We discussed the weather and the news from the front in a desultory fashion, and then, suddenly he leaned across the table and, with his mouth close to my ear, asked me if I too was "out there" with the "Vee-one". I effected what I hoped was a puzzled expression, but my companion persisted, beaming at me in a fatherly fashion and saying, "Come, come now. You can tell me, my friend. Are you flying over there again tomorrow?" I pretended to be even more puzzled, and the old gentleman whispered conspiratorially, "We all know what is going on. You are flying those Vee-Ones over the British coast, aren't you?" I shrugged my shoulders, and the old gentleman beckoned to the waiter and whispered in his ear, and then turning to me again and smiling, he said, "You don't have to tell me anything, but we can see it every day. Those things fly away and never come back, and they make such a frightful noise!" After the second bottle of wine from one of the finest vintages that I have yet had the pleasure of tasting, I knew for sure that I was "one of those fellows" who flew the Vee-Ones to the British coast and then baled out to be fished out of the channel by fast motor torpedo boats! As I staggered back to the airfield I thanked heaven that I could swim!

Our pinpoint landing instructions in the Stummel-Habicht gliders continued for a few days, but this interlude was soon over and the more serious side of our training began; thirty fledgling rocket pilots whose task was to be the operational testing of probably the most dangerous and volatile aircraft ever conceived— the Messerschmitt Komet. Our instructors were to be our commanding officer, Wolfgang Späte, his ever-cheerful shadow, Joschi Pöhs, his right-hand man, Toni Thaler, and courageous little Rudolf Opitz, popularly known as "Pitz". Wolfgang and "Pitz" were by far the "oldest" Komet pilots, not that they had so many years of flying experience but both had received their rocket education "first hand" so to speak at the Peenemünde test centre, and Joschi and Toni were also graduates of this most secret of schools.

The Komet's airframe and rocket power plant had already been extensively tested at Peenemünde alongside the equally revolutionary Vee-One and Vee-Two weapons, and now it was our turn. We were now to play our part in the gestation of one of the most awesome aerial weapons to be conceived, developing training procedures and operational tactics, and eventually providing the Gruppe and Staffel Leaders from our numbers once the Komet had attained large-scale production. It was obvious from the outset that the task assigned to Test Commando 16 was to be no picnic!

With the aid of lectures and films we new boys gradually learned everything that there was to know about the development of the Messerschmitt Me 163 to that time. We learned what had happened and, even more important, we learned what could still happen. Although it was never said in so many words, we were made all too aware of the fact that the rocket motor was highly temperamental; a take-off or a landing might provoke it into exploding, or it might explode without any provocation at any time! Constant experimentation had been conducted with the aim of eliminating this unpleasant possibility, but it had to be admitted that no means had been found to ensure that we would not be blown to kingdom come without so much as a second's warning. After all, if you smoke out a wasps' nest you must expect a few stings. Apart from this endearing characteristic, our instructors explained that it was virtually an everyday occurrence for the Komet's cockpit to fill with steam, almost completely obscuring the pilot's view, while fire was a serious hazard. In the event of fire, it was our duty, we were told, to extricate ourselves from the Komet's tiny shell just as quickly as possible, taking care to avoid hitting the vertical tail surfaces in the process.

As our instruction progressed we learned still more unpleasant facts of life, one of these being that we would do well not to depend too much on our special combination smocks supposed to protect us from burns resulting from fuel leaks. Should we forget to jettison our wheels after takeoff, or if these could not be dropped owing to some malfunctioning of the jettisoning gear, we were told that we should bail out as our chances of surviving a landing were on a par with finding the proverbial needle in a haystack. Again, if after a successful flight we found that we could not reach our airfield, then baling out was the only means of survival, for a landing on anything but our field would be suicidal.

With these admonitions, and explanations as to the purposes of all the levers, push-buttons, handles and instruments in the Komet's cockpit, our theoretical training was, for the moment at least, at an end. Much of what we had been told had passed above or through our heads, and few of us could truly have appreciated fully the risks involved in the task upon which we were now to embark, for only two of our number requested transfers to less dangerous hunting grounds.

Me 163A

Our practical training began with gliding flights in the Me 163A, the rocket fuel being replaced by ballast.

A twin-engined Messerschmitt Bf 110 served as our tug, the Me 163A being towed into the air at the end of a hundred metres of steel cable. Once airborne, the student in the cockpit of the Me 163A pulled a lever to jettison his wheels, climbed a few thousand metres behind the Bf 110 and then cast off the tow cable, gliding for a while to get the feel of the aeroplane before making his approach and endeavouring to land as near as possible to the cross marked on the airfield.

Eventually my turn came to clamber into the tiny cockpit of the Me 163A. The hood was slammed shut, I tested the controls, watched the cable tightening and, with a jerk, I was moving rapidly down the runway with the control column held dead straight. Then I was airborne, and as the wheels fell away I felt my lightly-loaded mount surge upward. At three thousand metres I cast off the cable, and I can remember few more exhilarating experiences than I enjoyed in the few minutes that followed. All the doubts and fears engendered by the ominous facts that we had learned seemed to leave me, and with sheer exuberance I threw my swift, silent mount around the sky. But all too soon a glance at my altimeter brought me to my senses, and I began my landing approach. I missed a heartbeat when the landing flaps dropped into position with a thump, turned carefully in preparation for aiming my aircraft at that ridiculous little cross in the middle of the field, and I was down to six hundred metres. A little right rudder . . . a clean sweep along the boundary . . . a gentle bank . . . level off . . . stick back slightly . . . and I had dropped on to the ground just behind the landing cross. I slithered along the ground, slowing rapidly. One wing dropped almost tenderly, and I came to a standstill.

I climbed from the cockpit with as much noncha-lance as I could muster, strolled across to some of my fellow pupils, and felt thoroughly pleased with myself. Some of the "bunch" were a little critical of my per-formance, but Toni Thaler said that it wasn't a bad landing for a first attempt, and that was good enough for me. At that moment, Toni called our attention to a "sharp" Me 163A that was being towed into position for a take-off at the other side of the field. A "sharp" Me 163A meant to us an aircraft with full fuel tanks and, naturally, we hurried across the field to get a closer view for, at that time, "sharp" take-offs had still to become an everyday sight.

Otto and Eli were hovering around the aircraft like mother hens, and Rudolf Opitz was strapping himself into the cockpit. The canopy was banged shut . . . there was a sharp crack . . . a momentary heat shimmer . . . and Pitz was accelerating down the runway, trailing a plume of smoke. The aircraft lifted off in seconds. The wheels fell away, rebounding from the runway and taking wild leaps across the field. Pitz pulled back on the stick and the aircraft shot upwards like a bat out of hell. Suddenly, at between two and three hundred metres, the rocket motor cut! A thick cloud of smoke blossomed from the tail of the aircraft which, climbing like an arrow a second before, immediately began to fall away. "Pitz! be careful, man!" Horror-stricken, we watched the grim scene which seemed to be taking place in slow motion. The fuel tanks were brim full; "Don't bank, man. She'll stall!" A gasp went around the group as Pitz began to bank his heavily loaded aircraft. I shut my eyes, tensed for the explosion that seemed inevitable, but, miracle of miracles, he had turned and was coming in low at twice the speed of an express train! Surely the fuel would blow the second his skid touched the runway, but no, as unpredictable as ever, there was still no explosion as Pitz touched down as lightly as a feather, throwing open the canopy as the aircraft slewed to a standstill. Then we were all around him, lifting him from his seat at the fire-fighting crew poured jets of water over the plane which was smoking menacingly. Pitz, pale and shaken, let out a low whistle of relief, shrugged his shoulders and, muttering something about his stars having looked kindly upon him that day, strolled off towards the mess. As we started to follow him, Toni pointed out most forcibly the inadvisability of any attempt on our part to emulate under similar conditions the low-level banking exhibition that we had just witnessed. "If it should happen to any one of you," Toni said, "pull the fuel quick-release handle at once and try to attempt a landing straight ahead—no banking and no turns."

"If at all possible, heading straight into the cemetery to save expenses," commented Fritz dryly.

Me 110

A few minutes later a Bf 110 trundled up, the pilot revving his engines, and our training was resumed. That evening, in the mess, we heard that Pitz's rocket motor had failed as a result of negative acceleration. It could have been the truth, it could have been an excuse. We had no way of telling, for such highly technical matters were hyper-secret. On the other hand, we already knew that negative acceleration more often than not resulted in an interruption in the fuel flow and, in consequence, the cutting of the rocket, but avoiding this was no simple problem. It was like telling a driver to maintain a constant 60 m.p.h. on a winding road but to avoid taking turns at speed. Whatever the cause of the failure of Pitz's rocket, it was indisputable that he had had a miraculous escape, and a riotous celebration of his good fortune in the mess that night left many of us with the feeling that we were loaded with that same highly volatile fuel that had so nearly led to his undoing.

3

A "Sharp" Start

WITH THE completion of our gliding course came the day when we fledglings had to make our first "sharp" starts. Some of our original scepticism, aggravated by Pitz's narrow escape, had been dispelled by a series of successful "sharp" starts demonstrated by Pitz, Späte, and Toni Thaler. Nevertheless, it was not without some misgivings that Fritz Kelb, who had been designated the first of us to make a "sharp" start, viewed the event and, before climbing into the cockpit, he fumbled in his pocket, pulled out a crumpled packet of cigarettes and handed it to me with the solemn words: "Here, Mano. There are three left. Smoke them in my memory if I get blown to pieces!"

But the Me 163A did not blow him to pieces, and I imagined that I could hear Fritz shouting for joy as he shot into the sky, followed by a violet-black trail of smoke. We saw the last of the stabbing flame from his perfectly functioning rocket motor as it drunk the dregs of the fuel, and then he was cavorting wildly about the sky high above our heads. Fritz's landing approach and touch-down were perfect and, while undoing his harness, he shouted to me: "Hey, Mano! I preferred that to taking out the most beautiful girl in Berlin!" And for Fritz to say that meant a *very* great deal.

17

And then it was my turn! I have never attempted
to break a wild horse in my life but were I to do so I am
sure that I should feel very much the same way as I did
before this first "sharp" start. I was afraid, that I could
not deny. I felt beads of perspiration forming on my
forehead, my mouth was dry and the palms of my
hands were sticky. I lowered myself into the cockpit. A
moment of panic and then the calm voice of my instructor giving me my instructions began to dissipate my
fears. "Keep the control column steady during take-off
. . . wait until you are a few metres off the ground and
drop your wheels . . . pull back a little on the stick as
you cross the airfield boundary . . . then let her climb
until all the fuel is gone." I was told that I should then
level off and begin a series of wide turns, gradually
tightening them but constantly watching my altitude,
and finally making a normal landing approach and
touching down. It all *sounded* so simple, but would that
blasted rocket motor behind me play along with the
game?

I trimmed slightly tail heavy, and with a last "Don't
forget your wheels!" ringing in my ears, the canopy was
slammed down and I was cleared for take-off. I quickly
checked the instruments and set the rocket control lever in the idling position to open the fuel cocks and
engage the starter motor. The system primed, my left
hand eased the control lever to full thrust and, much to
my surprise, the deafening roar from the rocket was
little more than a loud rustling sound in the cockpit!
Then the power of two thousand horses was pushing
me—no—chasing me across the field, faster and faster.
Suddenly the jolting and juddering ceased and I was
airborne. This was it! The rocket was snarling and
growling behind my back as I dropped my wheels, and
then, shoving me in the back, the little Me 163A tore
forward like an arrow from a bow. In a flash the airfield boundary was beneath me and I eased back a little
on the stick. Away we climbed like an express elevator,
and I was reclining on my back with nothing around
me but the infinite blue of the sky and a few strands of
cirrus far above. Superb! No other word can express

the pleasurable sensation as I shot ever upwards into the sky. My mind had been washed clean of all thoughts of danger and I could think of nothing but the beauty of flying and the joy of living. But more mundane matters soon intruded upon my reverie: the fine-course altimeter, the pressure gauges, the rev counter and other instruments to be watched. I had to prepare a report after this flight and it was essential that I watch these ridiculous dials and remember what they told me.

At this point there was a jerk and I felt as though I was swinging, suspended in mid-air. I sank forward in my harness, suddenly awakening to the fact that the growling behind me had stopped. The fuel was exhausted. Silence seemed to have descended around me like a soft curtain. The momentum of the aircraft carried it forward rapidly for a few hundred more metres and then the speed started to fall away. A glance at my altimeter told me that I was at four thousand metres and that I should start my wide turns. I dropped a wing and banked to starboard, seeing the Zwischenahn Lake glistening beneath me in the sunlight to bring back memories of happy days of sailing in more peaceful times. Well, I couldn't conceive the likelihood of having to ditch in that lake—our instructors had consoled us with the information that, in the event of ditching, our aircraft would sink like a stone and that we would have to be slippery indeed if we were not to accompany it to a watery grave. As far as I could see was spread a carpet of Friesian farmland, and it amused me to think that only a few days ago several of us were enjoying freshly smoked eel and large quantities of strong brandy in a little tavern nestling among those fields, but the stomach upsets the next day! Damned lucky that the weather that day had been QBI—or, to the uninitiated, "Absolutely Unfit for Flying!" It struck me that it was odd that my mind should meander in this fashion while I glided down to earth in a potentially lethal rocket plane. It *was* all too simple. I felt that something *should* happen—my elevons should jam suddenly, or one of the wing attachments should work itself loose. Perhaps I should be unable to find the airfield. But no, there it was, and I made my approach and landed as gently as some years earlier I had carried my young bride over the threshold of our home. I had found some affection for my spirited little Me 163A.

4

The "Powered Egg" Arrives

A HUMAN being can become used to anything—given time, be it a tedious daily office routine with an irrational and irritable boss or equally tedious sojourns in a low-pressure chamber and flights in a highly temperamental rocket plane. We were soon climbing into our Me 163As almost daily, although it would be hardly true to say that we did so with as little concern as we would have climbed into our car to go to the office. The low-pressure chamber had been made progressively less comfortable, and the good Doctor Dunker came in for much silent invective, although, later, we were to think more kindly of his efforts to ensure our altitude fitness. Whereas during the early stages of our training we had suffered nothing worse than a slow and comfortable series of pressure changes equivalent to a steady climb to eight thousand metres and down to sea level again, we were now rushed headlong to eight thousand metres in about a minute flat, hurtling down to sea level pressure in less than thirty seconds! During these terrific pressure changes our bowels felt as though they were expanding like balloons, forcing us to scream with agony, while if we happened to be suffering with a slight head cold and a blocked sinus, these sudden

pressure changes resulted in such searing head pains
that the agony was indescribable. It is true that Doctor
Dunker kept us under close and constant observation at
all times, and was quick to regulate the pressure in the
chamber when he saw that one of us was in difficulties,
but we could all think of preferable ways of passing our
time. However, we had the consolation of knowing that
our sufferings in the pressure chamber carried us nearer
to the day when our first Me 163B Komet—the true
"Powered Egg"—was scheduled to reach Test-Commando
16.

Around this time something happened that brought
us all down to earth with a resounding thump, and
those of us who were getting a little blasé over the
dangers that we were told confronted us had to adjust
our ideas. Although a very happily married man, I was
not averse to exchanging a smile or two with the occa-
sional pretty creature that appeared over the horizon,
but Bad Zwischenahn had one extremely attractive girl
to offer capable of extracting a smile from a confirmed
woman hater. Indeed, she was the darling of the unit,
and my admiring glances were by no means the only
ones enjoyed by Susanne, for that was her name. Then
fate took a hand. Susanne's fate was Joschi Pöhs.

Joschi, aide-de-camp to the C.O., was a handsome
specimen of manhood. Six feet in height, dark and
debonair, he sported a well-earned Knight's Cross, and
we all had to admit that he was everything that any girl
could wish for. Now, wherever Susanne was, there was
Joschi, escorting her like a beaming Apollo. The dice
had been cast so we retired gracefully to our respective
corners, all of us cherishing this romance. Our C.O.,
Wolfgang Späte, was still a hard-boiled bachelor, and
we could hardly expect him, therefore, to provide us
with a "First Lady" to act the rôle of hostess at the more
formal mess parties and functions, and in such circumstances it was the accepted thing that the wife or fiancée of the aide-de-camp should undertake these duties.
Why not Susanne? So we began a campaign aimed at
getting Joschi to announce officially his engagement as

soon as possible! The romance blossomed rapidly. Joschi and Susanne met every day. We saw them sailing together on the lake, strolling hand-in-hand on the beach or around the airfield, and in the Oldenburg Theatre in the evenings. And we liked what we saw! Soon we would have as attractive a "First Lady" as we could desire.

Me 163B Entering cockpit

And then, early one morning, Joschi climbed into the cockpit of an Me 163A and fastened his seat harness. It was to be just another routine flight like so many before, and Joschi, grinning and apparently without a care in the world, exchanged a joke or two with Pitz and Toni as they helped him with the various snap-fasteners and connections, shut his cockpit canopy and started his rocket engine. Since Pitz's hair-raising landing from a low-level turn nothing untoward had happened. All rockets had behaved with perfect respectability, and every "sharp" flight had been completed without hitch. But fate can be cruel and unpredictable, and it possessed an excellent tool in the Me 163A.

With a pulsating roar, Joschi's Me 163A ran across the grass field, rapidly gaining speed. It left the ground and the wheels dropped away but a fraction of a second later the heavy steel undercarriage chassis had rebounded from the ground and hit the aircraft! The rocket motor cut immediately, the bouncing chassis presumably having damaged the T-stoff feedline. How on earth could it have happened? Had the aircraft been too low or had the chassis struck an uneven patch of ground? Joschi must have realized what had happened at once for he pulled the nose of the aircraft up and, with the aid of his momentum, gained an altitude of about a hundred metres before banking steeply back towards the field just as Pitz had done that time! The aircraft appeared to be completely under control and we began to breathe again, thinking that with all his experience Joschi might pull it off. But he was coming dangerously close to one of the Flak towers of the airfield boundary. "Watch out, Joschi!" He couldn't hear us, of course, and in any case it was already too late for, his view apparently obscured by the wing, his aircraft grazed the tower. Such a slight touch, but more than enough. . . .

Now everything happened at once. Joschi's aircraft dropped like a stone, hit the airfield at an angle and skidded along the ground for some fifty metres before coming to a standstill. All this had taken place at least two kilometres from our flight line where we had been standing, and we ran as fast as our legs could carry us behind the racing fire tender and ambulance in the direction of the crippled aircraft. Surely it could not be too bad. Perhaps a few broken bones. At least there was no fire and no explosion! Both the fire tender and ambulance reached Joschi's machine within a minute of the crash, but our Joschi was no more. The T-stoff from the fractured fuel lines had seeped into the cockpit and poor Joschi, probably unconscious as a result of hitting his head on the instrument panel, had been literally dissolved alive! Nothing could have saved him.

Not even those thousands of gallons of water that the fire tender poured over the aircraft to neutralize that accursed T-stoff. It was already too late. Poor Susanne.

Joschi's death hit us hard, much harder than we would have believed possible after nearly four years of war; years in which we had lost more than enough of our comrades. But he was the first victim of the Me 163 from our midst, and he was the one and only Joschi!

5

Our First Casualty

ONE AFTERNOON some weeks later a rattling locomotive pulled a solitary sealed freight wagon along the airfield branch line and came to a standstill in front of the largest of our hangars. Like wildfire the news travelled around the airfield—our first Me 163B Komet had arrived at last!

As the seals on the wagon were broken and the doors pushed back we felt as though we were witnessing the opening of a newly-discovered tomb of some ancient Pharaoh. The atmosphere was electrifying; dark with secrecy and pregnant with expectation. It is improbable that any archaeologist staring for the first time on Egyptian treasures could have been more excited than we catching our first glimpse of the true "Powered Egg"! By the beard of Zeus, the Me 163B Komet was really something! Gone were the flattened rather ugly yet elegant contours of the Me 163A. There was nothing slender or ballerina-like about this newcomer. Yet the almost portly lines of the Komet somehow exuded power. Here was all the robustness of a dragon!

Larger than the Me 163A, the Komet was painted a vicious red all over, and its plexiglass canopy squatted atop its rotund body like an evil eye. It was no beauty in

26

the accepted sense, yet, again, it did possess beauty of a certain type; the beauty of a muscular wrestler. The sharply pointed nose enclosed a cone of fifteen-millimetre armour which, together with a ninety-millimetre armour-glass screen, gave frontal protection from enemy fire. Compared with that of the Me 163A, the Komet's cockpit was as spacious as a living room. In fact, the cockpit had proved *too* spacious, or so the manufacturers of the fighter had evidently concluded, for they had had the pleasing afterthought of installing a thirteen-gallon T-stoff tank on each side of the pilot's seat! "When this one explodes," someone muttered, "we will hit St. Peter in the eye as so much mincemeat!" The pilot's seat was fitted with a thirteen-millimetre armour segment for the protection of the head and shoulders, but the back of the seat, with its eight-millimetre armour slab, was, in effect, the firewall and all that divided the pilot from the unprotected T-stoff main tank with its two hundred-odd gallons! In fact, the happy pilot was seated within a frame of T-stoff tanks!

Whereas the semi-monocoque fuselage was built largely of light alloy with a dural stressed skin, the wings were single-spar units of wooden construction with plywood and fabric covering. This seemed fantastic for an aircraft designed to attain such speeds as those of the Komet. Both wings had fixed leading-edge slots, and as no horizontal tail surfaces were fitted, the control normally provided by a combination of elevators and ailerons was furnished by fabric-covered elevons. Inboard of these elevons were large trimming surfaces operated by a screw jack connected by linkage to a cockpit trimming wheel, and well forward of the trimming surfaces on the under-surface of each mainplane were simple split flaps of two-position type and operated by a hydraulic jack in the fuselage. Each wing housed fifty-five gallons of C-stoff which served as a catalyst and supplanted the Z-stoff of the Me 163A's engine. Below the cockpit was the hydraulically retractable landing skid, a shock-absorbing oleo leg being incorporated in the skid struts, and drain plugs were located in the base of the skid fairing to allow the fuel tanks to be flushed out after flight. The jettisonable two-wheeled dolly for take-off was attached to the rear portion of the landing skid by means of two lugs which engaged mechanical catches in the skid housing.

Now that we had our first showpiece and an object for contemplation, we had to get thoroughly acquainted with this new weapon, and we were soon learning a number of facts which, perhaps with clever foresight, had been withheld from us previously, or, for all we knew, had remained unknown even to our engineers until that time. Our engineers, Otto and Eli, were al- most boon companions, but I never attempted to delve into the intricacies of their profession and would not have done so even had they been willing to let me into their secrets. But at this juncture of my story perhaps I should make a confession. I had amassed many hun- dreds of hours in the air but I had never succeeded in arousing much interest in, for instance, the reason for a sparking plug packing up when one happens to turn the wrong screw inside the distributor. If it comes to that, I have never heard of anybody learning to ski from a knowledge of the manufacturing methods of skis themselves, nor have I met a pilot who, after an engine failure and before choosing a suitable spot for a crash landing, had time to regulate his ignition or to grind the valves! But now we began to receive concen- trated instruction in the theoretical side of rocket techniques, and I cannot say that I took kindly to this new stage in our training. So concentrated was this instruction that, in retrospect, the pre-examination stud- ies for my finals at high school began to look like the proverbial picnic.

We learned, for instance, that T-stoff was forty- eight per cent concentrated hydrogen peroxide and a mixture of hydrocarbon compounds, and that C-stoff was thirty per cent hydrazine hydrate solution in methyl alcohol. When the C-stoff was added to the T-stoff a decomposing reaction took place, resulting in tremen- dous thrust. The Walter HWK 109-509A rocket motor itself comprised an electric starter motor, a turbine, fuel pumps and pressure reducing valves. To start the

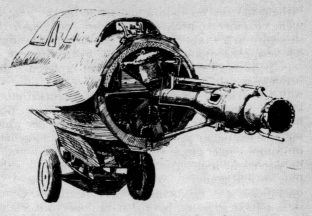

Me 163B Rocket motor: Walker HWK 109-590A

rocket the pilot pressed a push-button to activate the
electric motor which drove a small turbine to feed a
small quantity of T-stoff into the steam generator, the
steam being produced by the action of the catalyst,
calcium permanganate. The electric motor was then
switched off, and the turbine, driven by the steam
generator, began pumping T-stoff and C-stoff from
their respective tanks into a regulator unit at a ratio of
three to one. This ratio was maintained by the pressure-
reducing valves and then forced through twelve pipes
to the combustion chamber. The combustion chamber
itself was a double-walled cylindrical unit, the inner
wall terminating in a venturi. Combustion was con-
trolled by the main chamber control valve which, in
turn, was activated by a single lever in the pilot's cockpit which regulated the flow of T-stoff and C-stoff, the
latter being pre-heated by circulation around the cool-
ing jacket of the combustion chamber. The control
lever had five positions: off, idling, and first, second
and third thrust stages. The weight of the rocket motor
was only 365 pounds, and the total fuel supply of 336
gallons was consumed in four or five minutes. The
maximum thrust was no less than 3,750 pounds, yet the

turbine was smaller than a margarine packet, and the
main chamber control, or regulator, could easily be
slipped into a trouser pocket! Truly a mighty midget.
The complete motor was attached to the airframe by
four bolts and could be removed and replaced within
two hours.

Before being cleared for flight, every rocket motor
had to undergo functional tests in the airframe. Both
T-stoff and C-stoff tanks were filled with water which
then passed under pressure through the steam generator into the inlet pipes. If all inlet pipes were found to
be watertight and all tanks completely empty within
four to five minutes, then the engine was passed for
operational use. Fortunately, both T-stoff and C-stoff
were soluble in water, but the most dangerous was the
T-stoff which was ablaze at the slightest contact with
any organic substance. Therefore, before any rocket
motor could be run or any "sharp" start made, a fireman had to be standing by with a running hose in
order to neutralise any fuel leaks immediately. It can
well be imagined how the interior of the rocket motor
test hangar looked when these power plants, both on
test benches and in airframes, were undergoing "cold"
and "hot" runs. It was a witch's cauldron; a bubbling,
steaming, hissing, fire-spitting wash-house in which one
could not tell the difference between a Major and a
chimney sweep. The noise was colossal; pounding against
the ear drums in a searing frenzy until one could no
longer hear oneself think! Just a brief sojourn in the
"rocket laundry" was enough to result in frayed tempers.
But it was all so new and interesting that we could
hardly wait for the day to dawn when we would fly
these "devil's sledges" for the first time.

One of our pastimes during this period took the
form of standing around the "hot" engine test banks. It
was, of course, impossible to run a "hot" engine full
blast in a closed hangar, and therefore the rear wall of
the "rocket laundry" had a number of apertures cut in
it, the effluxes of the rockets under test being pushed
against these so that the jet streams blasted away outside the hangar. If one stood within ten or twenty

metres of these apertures while the rockets were running it would have been tantamount to committing
suicide, but for some time we amused ourselves by
standing a hundred metres or so from these openings
when the rockets were going full blast. We were all in
possession of rubber ear plugs to protect our ear drums
from the unbearable noise, and it was not an unpleasant sensation to feel the hot waves of air from the
rocket jet pounding against the stomach. To add to
the interest, we took it in turns to see how near to the
flame-spitting holes we could walk before the heat
became too intense.

The handling of T-stoff and C-stoff demanded
some very special precautions. Both fluids were colourless
and, for this reason, the tanks and the buckets that
housed them were painted in different colours. Some
time earlier, at Peenemünde, an unfortunate mechanic
had poured a few litres of C-stoff into a bucket containing some dregs of T-stoff. He didn't live long enough
to realize what he had done, but his carelessness probably saved others, for the mistake was never repeated.
T-stoff could only be kept in aluminum containers, as
steel or iron tanks rapidly disintegrated while rubber-
ized containers, like anything else made of organic
matter, burst into flame immediately. All T-stoff feedlines
and feedline connections were manufactured from an
artificial fibre known as Mipolam, and every T-stoff
container had to be carefully sealed as the smallest dust
particles or insects could set off a reaction which would
blow the tank to smithereens. C-stoff, on the other
hand, could only be kept in glass, enamel or anodically-
treated containers, this fluid corroding anything made
of aluminum.

During this time we had a welcome visit from that
fabulous woman pilot, Hanna Reitsch. She did not come
to Bad Zwischenahn merely to pass the time of day,
either, but to fly! Very few of us knew Hanna personally,
but it was common knowledge among us pilots that this
courageous girl had suffered terrible injuries when she
had crashed in an Me 163 at Regensburg a year earlier,

and that it had taken a tremendous amount of medical skill and an iron will on the part of Hanna to overcome the effects of the accident. And now this same Hanna was standing with us on the flight line, pulling herself into the cockpit of an Me 163A, joining us in the low-pressure chamber or the "rocket laundry" and, in fact, living among us like a soldier among other soldiers. Yet there was nothing masculine about Hanna. She was quite a delicate creature and could laugh as gaily as any young girl. Only her eyes betrayed her iron will and the fantastic inner strength and energy belied her slight body, and every time we helped her into the cockpit of an Me 163 and gave her a hand with the fastening of her seat straps we could not help being affected by so much keenness and courage.

At the same time, we were all anxious for her safety. It was not that we considered these rocket planes to be our prerogative alone. It was merely that we were men and Hanna was a woman. Again, Hanna was not just any woman—she was the one and only Hanna Reitsch, a symbol of German womanhood and the idol

Me 163B

of German aviation. But Hanna did not seem to be aware of our fears and anxieties, nor of the fact that we all now turned up for our duties as immaculate as if we were about to be inspected by our general. She was a pilot, body and soul. Men and women as such simply did not exist for Hanna. There were only pilots and "others"!

Shortly after Hanna's arrival the first "sharp" start was made with the Me 163B Komet, Wolfgang Späte himself making this first test. It was a delightful winter morning. The airfield had a light crusting of fresh snow as pure and fine as icing sugar and upon which the sun sparkled as though on a myriad of jewels. The winter sky was radiantly blue, and little columns of smoke were climbing lazily into the sky from the chimneys of nearby Zwischenahn and from the antiquated local train puffing along the track on its way to Oldenburg.

The preparations for a rocket take-off were still quite a procedure. The pilot climbed up a small ladder, lowered himself into the cockpit, shifted the parachute pack into a comfortable position beneath his posterior, and then allowed one of the ground crew to force the stiff harness belts over his bulging combination suit. He then checked the instruments—his last chance to do so without goggles and with a "free nose", connected the R/T leads from his helmet to the FuG radio, switched on the necessary electrical instruments (generator, reflector sight, pitot tube heating, etc.), tested the control surfaces and flaps for free movement, and turned the trim wheel to set trim three degrees tail heavy. Then he placed his oxygen mask in position and checked the flow and, at the same time, his "number one" closed the cockpit canopy which had to be locked from the inside. He was then ready for take-off.

We stood silently watching this procedure on the morning that Späte was to take the Komet up for the first powered flight from our field. Finally, our C.O. gave the "thumbs up" to indicate that he was ready to go, and his "number one" switched on the starter trailer and the turbine began to howl like an abandoned fox terrier. Then the starter trailer was dragged clear, there was a sharp crack as fuel sprayed into the combustion chamber. The white steam disappeared, a brief gurgling, and then, with a roaring stab of flame patterned with shock waves, the Komet began to wobble forward like a duck on dry land. Suddenly, it shot forward with a deafening roar, and our eager eyes followed the bright red machine as it shot across the field like a phantom, jumped slightly and was airborne. So far, so good. The Komet gained about ten metres altitude and Späte dropped his wheels, which danced away in a wild jig while the fighter, relieved of their weight and drag, sped away like an arrow. It streaked across the airfield boundary, the nose came up and it was tearing into the blue on the end of a silvery white trail. What a spectacle! Our eyes followed the tiny fighter until it disappeared from sight, and then we scanned the skies for the contrail that would betray its position ten or twelve thousand metres above us. A thin white pin-line appeared against the clear blue winter sky. A few minutes later, a shout drew our attention to a tiny speck, growing larger rapidly, until Späte whistled across the airfield and, using the momentum gained in his dive, and without any help from the rocket motor which had already exhausted its fuel, soared up into the sky again. This time we managed to keep it in sight, and watched Späte perform a series of wide turns, gradually tightening them as he lost altitude, until he levelled off, made a perfect approach, touched down softly and slid across the newly fallen snow.

Späte was still sitting in the cockpit, smiling happily, when we reached the Komet, but he was unable to move—his fingers had frozen stiff inside their gloves and he could neither release his harness or lift himself from the seat. He was as helpless as a baby, and it was fortunate that there was no need for him to make a hurried exit. We lifted him from the cockpit and rubbed his fingers with snow as he told us of the flight, although to listen to Späte one might have thought that this first test of the Me 163B was an everyday routine matter.

*   *   *

We were overjoyed by the success of Späte's flight, and could hardly contain ourselves until the day that we too would climb into the cockpit of the Komet for a "sharp" start. The weather remained fine, one beautiful day following another, and during this period several more operational Me 163B fighters arrived, and the flame-spitting rocket test stands were constantly active. We continued our gliding flights in the Me 163A, towed into the air behind a Bf 110, but this seemed tame now, and we were increasingly eager to complete this phase of our training and get to grips with the real "Powered Egg".

A certain Sergeant Alois Wörndl from Aschau, an excellent fellow and completely reliable, flying with the accuracy of a precision instrument, was chosen from among us pupils to make the first "sharp" start in the Komet. "Make it good, Alois!" we shouted, and then he was off. To make our first "sharp" take-offs in the Komet *less* dangerous the fuel tanks were not filled to the brim, although, in our opinion, a few hundred litres one way or another did not much affect the odds—it was still T-stoff! Of course, this meant that the Komet could not get up to its full operational altitude and remained within our sight throughout the test. As expected, Alois's rocket motor cut at about six thousand metres altitude, and he turned back towards the airfield, gliding down according to instructions, as precise as ever. We could see the Komet flattening out preparatory to landing, and then, without warning, "Sideslip!" The shout came from one of the group. We could now all see only too clearly that Alois was much too high to touch down anywhere near the landing cross! "Sideslip, Sideslip!" We all shouted as if he could hear us, but the Komet shot past us—and the landing cross! Too high, too fast! We watched with horror as it floated away across the airfield as though some invisible hand was holding the aircraft away from the safety of the runway. Anxiously we watched the Komet touch down far outside the airfield perimeter, rebound into the air, drop back again like a brick, and then skid into

some rough ground and turn over on its back. A split
second later a blinding white flame shot up, followed
by a mushroom of smoke!

The fire tender and the ambulance were already
racing in the direction of the disaster as I jumped
aboard our already-accelerating servicing lorry. At top
speed we raced towards the growing mushroom of oily
black smoke, and my mind's eye saw a picture of Alois's
happy face a few minutes before as we had strapped
him into the Komet's cockpit. "Hold tight!" shouted the
driver as, with his foot hard down on the accelerator,
we bounded across some rough ground. I nearly lost
my precarious hold on the door frame as my feet
bounced off the running board, but I clung on desperately. We were still about a kilometre from the scene of
the crash, and I could see that the fire tender had
already arrived and its crew were pouring streams of
water over the wreckage. "Watch out for the axles!"
somebody shouted as we hurtled across the rough
ground on the far side of the perimeter track. "To hell
with the axles!" someone else shouted in reply. We were
still some five hundred yards from the wreckage, and
the flames were beginning to subside under the jets
from the hosepipes. I jumped from the still-moving
lorry and ran towards the smoking, hissing debris. About
twenty yards away the ambulance attendants were lifting Alois's body on to a stretcher.

It seemed that Alois had been thrown from his seat
when his aircraft hit the ground for the second time,
and his neck and both legs had been broken instantaneously. At least he had died quickly. Late that afternoon I was told to report to Späte's office. "Ziegler,
Wörndl's relatives would like to have his body returned
to his home. I wish you to act as escort for the coffin,
together with Corporal Glogner. Give my deepest sym-
pathy to his parents." Späte's voice sounded odd, his
eyes seemed tired and his lips were compressed tightly.
He asked me if I had any questions. I replied, "Yes, Sir!
Why did Wörndl overshoot today? His landings have
always been so perfect!" Späte shrugged his shoulders.
"Possibly too much fuel left in his tanks. The fireworks

after the crash made it look that way. Perhaps he miscalculated and came in too fast, perhaps . . ." He was silent for a moment and then continued bitterly: "We must have a means of quickly jettisoning the fuel! It is vital! I am told that something is being done about this on later aircraft, but it is no simple problem. The aperture must be large enough to empty the tanks in a few seconds!" Then he nodded and I was dismissed.

In the early morning twilight on the following day, we lifted the coffin tenderly into a railway wagon and laid wreaths over it. Sergeant Wörndl was ready for his last journey home. The company presented arms—their last tribute to their comrade, and Rolf Glogner and I scrambled into the wagon. This usually happy-go-lucky corporal from Berlin had little to say throughout the journey, and nibbled dejectedly at the end of a cigarette. In the luggage rack were our two kitbags and Alois's possessions in two suitcases, and a shiver ran down my spine as the thought struck me that one day those suitcases on the rack might contain my belongings, and two comrades would be sitting silently in our places. As if he had read my thoughts, Glogner said: "Will you take *me* home when it happens, Lieutenant?" His voice roused me from my morbid thoughts. "Or the other way around," I replied. "All this makes no sense to me," Glogner added. "First Pöhs and now Wörndl! All this without a fight, without anything! At this rate, I am beginning to wonder how many of us will be left to take the Komet into combat!" "Maybe so, Glogner," I replied, "but if it comes to that what difference does it make if we go down this way or get chopped down by some Englishman. Once you're dead you're dead!" But the young corporal, who could nearly have been my son, didn't agree. "I want to know why when I get the chop! There is a hell of a difference between having a good scrap with a Spitfire up there and ending up by providing a billet for a bullet, and making a ridiculous landing like Wörndl's and breaking your bloody neck!"

Two days later the coffin containing Alois Wörndl's mortal remains was slowly lowered into the rocky soil of

Aschau cemetery. Down in the valley between the silent
mountains sparkled the silvery-blue waters of the
Chiemsee Lake, and over the small village churchspire
rose the steep and mighty Kampenwald rock. Alois
Wörndl was home.

Spitfire

6

Späte's Narrow Escape

FOR SOME time after Wörndl's unfortunate accident the top priority problem at Bad Zwischenahn was this matter of dumping the fuel quickly in an emergency. Späte himself was the first of us to climb into a brand new Komet just out of the works to try out an emergency dumping system devised by the Messerschmitt people. The fuel could, they told us, be jettisoned by turning a cock on the left of the main instrument panel.

With bated breath, we followed Späte's shining white contrail across the sky and waited impatiently for him to land. The landing cross had been laid out in exactly the same way as when Wörndl went down for the last time. Späte crossed the airfield at an altitude of about a thousand metres and then turned in and started to glide down for his landing approach. Once again we screamed "Sideslip!" but this time, as though he could hear us, the chief dropped his port wing and righted the aircraft. He carefully levelled off, raised the nose a little, and, yes, a perfect landing . . . but, no! Späte shot past us. We knew that his tanks could be nowhere near empty! He was much too fast and had already overshot the landing cross. This was Wörndl's landing all over again! The Komet leapt into the air, hit the ground with a rending crash, bounced up again, and then skid-

39

ded across a ploughed field, throwing up sods of earth.
It stopped with a jerk and the tail lifted high. This was
the end! The explosion had to come any moment as
soon as the aircraft flipped on to its back. But somehow
the impossible happened. The Komet stood on its nose
for a few seconds, and then, slowly, it settled back on its
belly!

We were already clambering on to the servicing
lorry, and in the distance we saw the chief jump from
the cockpit as if every devil in hell was under his seat,
and race pell-mell away from the aircraft which was
exuding an ominous cloud of steam. In less time than it
takes to tell, the fire tender was swamping the aircraft
with water, and the danger had passed. Späte himself
didn't say a word when we reached him. He simply
stared at the fire tender and then at the quick-release
cock that he held in his hand. The cock was a mock-up!
The damned aircraft had no dumping system at all!
Somebody had slipped up very badly, and his ears must
have burned as though they had T-stoff in them!

We had begun to get used to unpleasant surprises
like this, and after our immediate fury was spent we
could discuss the whole situation objectively. The fact
that a large amount of fuel had still been left in the
tanks after the rocket motor had cut no longer occa-
sioned much surprise. These dregs could blow the aircraft and pilot to Hades after a perfectly normal landing,
and they were to force many a fighter pilot to bale out
of his Komet in a hell of a hurry within sight of the
enemy and without firing a shot!

We drove over to the big hangar where Oertzen
and Otto Böhner, who, after Joschi's death, had taken
over as technical officer, were just about to examine
Späte's damaged aircraft. The rocket motor had apparently cut at eight thousand metres, but there had still
been plenty of fuel in the tanks, and the reason that
this fuel had not been burned was not readily apparent.
The T-stoff containers occupied practically the whole
of the fuselage ahead of the rocket motor and, consequently, the feed pump could not be fitted beneath

these tanks which would have been the most efficient way of ensuring that the tanks were pumped dry. It was eventually concluded that this was the reason. Attempts were made to empty the tanks by using a system of pipe-bends, and this was quite successful when the motor was being run on the test stand, all the fuel being burned in "one go". Unfortunately, the system did not function so well under actual flight conditions. When the Komet was let loose with full tanks and maximum pressure, it shot up to over fifteen thousand metres altitude, and as none of our aircraft was equipped with pressure cabins this was impossible. On the other hand, if the pilot levelled off at a safe altitude and then attempted to fly under full power, the Komet quickly experienced compressibility. But if one attempted to throttle the rocket motor while climbing to a given altitude and then levelling off, it was on the cards that negative acceleration would cause bubbles in the feedlines and result in the motor cutting while substantial quantities of fuel remained in the tanks. We seemed to be in a cleft stick!

Otto and Eli rolled up their sleeves and worked furiously, and Böhner chewed his already shaggy beard while trying to master the problem—Späte was determined to have an answer, and quickly! That same afternoon a second Komet stood outside the big hangar awaiting our chief. He *knew* that this one had no fuel dumping installation, but he wanted to examine the problems of negative acceleration and to evolve some preventive measure without delay, for we pupils were coming up for our "sharp" starts in the Komet.

The take-off was perfectly normal, and Späte's Komet was soon streaking up into the sky. It disappeared from view and then we spotted his contrail which seemed to be at a much greater altitude than on the earlier flight. Soon he was plumeting down like a meteor, and then circled the field a couple of times before making his final approach. Again we held our breath. He touched down perfectly but now the frozen grass allowed him to continue skidding across the field at tremendous speed! The Komet gave no sign of slowing down and was rapidly approaching the perimeter! And then something totally unexpected happened. The cockpit canopy flew off and Späte's body whirled through the air, striking the wing and then bouncing on the ground, the aircraft careering on at more than a hundred kilometres per hour! I noticed a mechanic beside me make the sign of the cross and, metaphorically, I did also. At that moment the runaway aircraft turned over on its back and disappeared in a brilliant flash debris being thrown in every direction.

We found Späte lying unconscious on the frozen ground, a thin trickle of blood running from the back of his head. "Hell, I've seen too much for one day," muttered Fritz Kelb, as they carried the chief away. "He was a bloody fool to try it twice today!"

"Leave the chief alone," somebody replied. "He knows what he is doing, and let's thank the Lord that we didn't get one of those bloody chairborne warriors as a commanding officer!"

While we were at supper in the mess, Hilda Dyckerhoff, the wife of the senior staff doctor, telephoned to tell us that the chief was in not too bad a state, all things considered. He had suffered bad concussion, but he hadn't cracked his skull. I took the call and Hilda suggested that if I was not doing anything I might care to visit her, taking Langer and Kelb with me. She mentioned that Hanna Reitsch would be there. The Dyckerhoffs' house stood in Bad Zwischenahn, a haven never forgotten by any of our number that enjoyed an evening there. And it was not so much Helmut Dyckerhoff's wine cellar or Hilda's superlative cooking. It was the delightfully restful atmosphere that seemed to surround these charming people.

It was not my first visit to Hilda and Helmut, and both Fritz and Herbert felt just as much at home there as I did. The Dyckerhoffs had taken us to their hearts and accepted us as their equals despite the fact that they were nearly old enough to be our parents, and we called them "Madam Doctor" and "Sir" nearly as familiarly as we might have said "Aunt" or "Uncle". In joy or sorrow, Hilda never lost her Viennese charm. "Well, what do you think of Späte?" These were the first words with which she greeted us as we entered the house. "He has been exceptionally lucky. Yes, very lucky! It is amazing that he could jump from the aircraft at that speed, let alone survive the experience. I think I should have stayed in the seat and closed my eyes!"

"Had you done so it would have been for ever!" commented Fritz Kelb.

Doctor Dyckerhoff arrived home shortly afterward from Oldenburg. "Späte sends his warmest greetings," he said, "and told me to tell you to drink a bottle of something decent to celebrate his good fortune." He then fetched a bottle of something very decent indeed, and we duly toasted our chief. We heard that Späte had fully regained consciousness while still on the way to the hospital, and had immediately started abusing all and sundry. There was nothing the matter with him, he told them, and insisted that they took him straight back to the field. The doctor told us that he had said: "How would you like to climb straight into another Komet? A few more burst blood vessels in your brain won't matter much one way or the other now!" But Späte soon saw the light, and to the good doctor's suggestion that he should spend the next four weeks flat on his back, he made a counter offer of fourteen days. After much arguing a period of three weeks was agreed upon.

During Späte's absence Pitz took over Test-Commando 16, and got us through our "sharp" take-offs in the Komet one after another. For nearly three weeks everything went smoothly apart from one accident. It was an abortive start, and the Me 163B broke away immediately, skidding over the field in wide turns, but the pilot was lucky, succeeding in jumping clear just before the aircraft blew up. Apart from this incident, our days were remarkably trouble-free, and Späte returned to us after precisely three weeks in hospital. Needless to say, we celebrated his return with a memo-

rable evening in the mess, and the next day the chief
was on his way to see the General of Fighters in Berlin.

It was just after Späte had left for Berlin that an
event occurred which brought us up sharp, underlining
the frightful destructive power of the Komet. Shortly
before lunch an Me 163B was being made ready for a
routine start on the flight line, and the mechanics were
busy with their last-minute checks. In the meantime, we
had gone into the mess, and Walter, who was to fly this
particular Me 163B, had hurried past on his way to the
aircraft. Pitz called after him that he would join him on
the flight line in ten minutes, and hardly ten minutes
had elapsed when we strolled out of the mess and
headed for the flight line. The workshop vehicle with
the starter passed us as we walked towards the Komet,
and Pitz was just telling us about a new pressure suit
that was supposed to be tested very soon and should, if
it worked, enable us to attain much greater operational
altitudes, when a fantastic hiss followed immediately by
the whiplash of an explosion interrupted our conversation, and seemed to tear the air in pieces around us.
For a split second we were rooted to the spot. The
Komet had exploded on the flight line!

"Walter!"—somebody shouted. Then we were all
running in the direction of the flight line as fast as our
flying suits and fur boots would allow. A frightful sight
met our eyes. Where only a minute or so earlier a
Komet had stood ready for take-off there was now nothing but a dark, smoking stain on the ground! Scattered
in a rough circle hundreds of metres in diameter were
scraps of twisted tubing, distorted pieces of metal—all
that was left of a brand new fighter. The bile rose in
our throats as we saw a few traces of bloody sinews and
a snow-white piece of bone stuck to a jagged piece of
metal that may have come from the cockpit. Then one
of the mechanics called us to a spot about eighty metres
away from the center of the explosion—he had discovered a naked leg ripped off just below the knee. This
was all that was left of our Walter!

How could this tragedy have happened? There was

no way in which an explanation could be ascertained—
there was not enough of the Komet left! Possibly some
feedline had developed a leak—perhaps a minute hole,
but one large enough to allow Death to push in her
bony finger! Never before had we realized how awesome was the power of this rocket fuel when it chose
the way of violence rather than usefulness. We just
stood around in silence, feeling anger, nausea and fear,
and the most appalling helplessness. Medical personnel
came along and placed Walter's leg and that solitary
fragment of bone on a stretcher. They searched the
area carefully for another fifteen minutes, but there
was nothing more to find. Then they lifted the stretcher
with those pathetic human relics, placed it carefully
into the ambulance and drove away. To keep our minds
occupied, we began gathering the pieces of Walter's
Komet, trying to guess where each scrap came from. A
few heavier pieces were lifted on to a lorry, and that
was that!

Late that afternoon I was assigned to the task of
listing Walter's personal belongings. A sergeant was
sent to assist me. A photo of a pretty girl; a packet of
letters; a picture of his brother wearing the Iron Cross
and enclosed by a silver frame crossed with black
crepe . . . ! In a loud voice I itemized everything for
the sergeant who was making the list: "Eight handkerchiefs—four pairs of socks—one pair of civilian trousers,
brown with white stripes—four singlets. . . ." When the
small suitcase was packed, I thought to myself that
there was still room for all that remained of Walter
himself. Et tu, Mano! What I needed was a stiff drink.

Next morning I went to see the chief, who in the
meantime had returned from Berlin. I had to report
on the preparations for Walter's funeral, but on my
way to his office I met Hanna Reitsch just leaving. Did
she have tears in her eyes—or was I mistaken? With
barely a nod, she brushed past me—and that wasn't a
bit like Hanna. Späte seemed nervous and ill at ease
when I entered his office. The atmosphere seemed
heavy with foreboding, but perhaps I was imagining it.

The tragic event of the day before had cast gloom over the whole airfield. I saluted and made my report.

"Thank you, Lieutenant," barked Späte, "but this time somebody else will have to escort the coffin. You are scheduled to make your first 'sharp' take-off in the Komet at 10.00 hours tomorrow. Weather permitting, you will be the first one on the line!"

"Yes, Sir!"

"Your aircraft will be ready tonight, Lieutenant. Captain Opitz will fly it first, and then it will be your turn. You may feel like going to a concert tonight. Beethoven's Third, I believe. You'll find two tickets in my name at the box office."

"Thank you, Major!"

Hanna Reitsch

I left his office and began looking for Hanna. Perhaps a concert would cheer her up. I eventually learned that she was in her quarters. I knocked on her

door, but it was only after my third knock that she
replied. I went in, and there was Hanna, crying her
eyes out on her bed!

"For goodness sake, what's the matter, Hanna?"
She made no secret of her grief, and made no attempt
to stop the flow of tears. Eventually she mumbled:
"Späte has forbidden me to fly tomorrow, and it was all
arranged! Oh, it's all so mean!"

So that was it! I felt more at ease. Hanna continued:
"He knows very well that I have longed for this take-off
ever since my accident. And now he slams the door in
front of my nose. It is so unfair!"

I asked her why Späte had suddenly decided not to
allow her to fly the Komet.

"It could be *too* dangerous! He says that he is not
prepared to take the responsibility in case something
should happen to me. As if I have ever asked if a flight
will be dangerous or not! It is just because I am a
woman! Oh no! Women are not good enough to fly the
Komet!"

"But you have flown it before, Hanna," I said,
hoping to pacify her a little, her heartrending sobs
leaving me more than a little discomforted.

"Towed starts only—do you call *that* flying?"

"But you have made rocket take-offs in the Me
163A, haven't you?"

"Of course I have, but the 'A' is not the 'B', and I
want . . . I will fly the 'B'! I shall go straight away to see
Goering—today, now!"

She got up and began throwing things into suitcases.
Her tears had stopped now, and there was a hard glint
in her eyes. It was obvious to me that, following the last
tragic accident, Späte was determined not to allow this
unique woman to risk her life at any price. Her name
was almost legendary in aviation circles. But Hanna was
determined that she *would* fly the Komet and assist us
in its development even if she had to appeal to the
highest in the land. She had a will of iron and she was
not beaten yet. She would overcome Späte's squeamish-
ness one way or another. She slammed her suitcases
shut, and said: "Give my heartfelt regards to all our

comrades, Mano. Thank them all for the wonderful days that I have spent here with them at Bad Zwischenahn. I shall never forget them!"

And so Hanna Reitsch left Test-Commando 16. She was sorely missed by us all.

7

A Pleasant Interlude

So I was stuck with two tickets for a concert which it looked as though I would have to attend on my own. Herbert was duty officer and had also been ordered to make the preparations for Walter's funeral, so he could not accompany me, but I didn't want to go alone. Not that evening of all evenings! Fritz Kelb appeared on the scene, but at my suggestion that he should join me, he said something to the effect that Beethoven was too heavy going for him. Finally he had idea—how about Helga? He said that he was sure that she would enjoy a concert and that, if I had no objection, he would telephone her on my behalf.

For several weeks Helga had been Herbert's girlfriend. She had a job in Oldenburg, and Herbert had met her at a "get-together" dance given by the Oldenburger Fusiliers. Now it was only a question of time. Herbert was awaiting his next leave so that he could take Helga to his Silesian home, introduce her to his family and become formally engaged. They made a fine pair. It was one of those natural matches for everybody could only wish every happiness in the future.

It was sheer pleasure escorting Helga to the concert that evening. She was radiantly beautiful in a silver brocade dress over which she wore a blue velvet cape. I was grateful to have such an excellent reason for dressing myself up in my "number one" uniform. From Helga's home it was but a short walk to the concert hall, and I was soon in the best of spirits with no qualms for the morrow. The first movements of the Eroica were soon embracing me and I was completely lost to the world of exploding rocket planes and sudden death. The conductor lowered his baton, and the audience breathed freely again.

After a short interval, the Funeral March began to spread its dark and gloomy wings over the concert hall—hardly an item that I should have chosen for this particular evening. I no longer found it possible to lose myself in the music. A little voice somewhere in my mind kept saying, "Make the most of it, Mano! Tomorrow may be your turn!" I glanced at Helga, trying to blot out this mocking whisper in my mind, but it was no good. "Maybe you'll never get airborne, Mano! Perhaps you will be shaking hands with Joschi, Alois and Walter this time tomorrow!"

I had intended to go straight back to Bad Zwischenahn so that I should get as much sleep as possible but, as I assisted Helga with her cape, a loudspeaker crackled into life and informed us that an enemy bomber formation was approaching Oldenburg. We hurried from the concert hall and reached a small wine tavern just as the sirens began their dirge. Together with several other customers, our host led us down to the cellar which, to my surprise, proved to be a very comfortable room. He did not allow the sirens to affect his duties as a host, and served us with a real grandezza—red wine and small cheese sandwiches. We might have been sitting in the bar of some hotel in Palermo!

"I hope that these raids will come to an end when your planes are ready for action," Helga sighed. "How I wish that it was all over!"

"We'll make it," I replied, but perhaps my voice did not carry much conviction for she immediately said: "But do you *really* believe in these wonder weapons?"

"Of course I do!" I replied. But had I then had to swear on a Bible I could not have said if I was lying or telling the truth. "We've got them anyway," I added lamely, "and they may be of decisive importance some day!"

"If it is not too late already!"

"It is never too late, Helga!" I said. "Only sometimes it is not soon enough! You have heard it yourself tonight—that furious, stormy first movement, followed by the deep mourning of the second, brightening a little here and there. But the second movement is followed by the third, and the fourth. . . !"

"Like the Second World War followed the First?"

Anxious to change the subject, I suggested that we should drink Herbert's health. At that moment the sirens sounded the all clear, and we left the tavern. I just had time to catch the last train back to Bad Zwischenahn, and Helga hurried with me to the station. "Thanks for a lovely evening!" she shouted as the train started moving, and I found myself alone in a cold, dark compartment. But the wine had done its work well. I glanced up at the star-filled, cloudless night sky. Yes, I would be up there tomorrow. It would be a piece of cake. My rocket motor would function perfectly and drain the last drop of T-stoff from the tanks. Twenty minutes later the train jerked to a halt. "Baaaad Zwischenahn"—the familiar voice of the station-master shouted in the darkness, and I trudged up the road towards our private world hidden behind those fences of barbed wire.

I had the shock of my life when I opened the door of my room and switched on the light. My bed was in a heap on the floor. My pyjama trousers were hanging from the lampshade, and the jacket was swinging from the curtain rail. My shaving brush was floating in an old jam jar, the toothbrush was protruding from a pot of ink, and shirt-collars, handkerchiefs and other items had been attached to the ceiling with drawing pins! On the table was a large cardboard sheet inscribed "A soldier must lock his quarters—he must surrender his key

at the guard house—he must not hang about so long
with somebody else's fiancée! Goodnight, Lieutenant,
Sir!—Herbert and Fritz." After having made sure that
my chair had not been doctored with mustard or shaving cream, I sat down and had a good laugh. "Oh,
yes, vengeance will be mine!" I thought, but I was
too tired to plan any just retribution, and so I repaired
the worst of the ravages of my uninvited guests and
turned in.

It must have been a very bad dream that woke me
at 06.00 hours. I lay there for a while, wrestling with
the thought that in a few hours it would be my turn to
climb into the Komet for a "sharp" start. The palms of
my hands were sticky; cold water seemed to be trickling
down my spine. Fear was sitting on my pillow. I jumped
from my bed, splashed cold water over my face, and
began to feel better. Back in bed once more, I soon fell
asleep and would almost certainly have overslept had
not curiosity drawn Herbert and Fritz back to the "scene
of their crime".

"Come on! Off that bed. Your one-six-three is steaming and ready to blow already!" I staggered out of bed,
and Herbert said: "How was the concert?"

"Oh, we didn't go to the concert," I replied.

"Where the hell did you go to then?"

"Well, we went back to Helga's place. Her parents
are away, you see, so I took along a bottle of sekt and
we enjoyed it together. It was quite an evening!"

"You're a lying b——," screamed Herbert.

"And then, when the air raid alarm sounded,
Helga and I went down to the cellar. Quite comfortable down there. We were all alone, too! Of course,
we found a bottle of liqueur to comfort us. Oh yes,
I nearly forgot. Helga asked me to tell you, Herbert,
that she will not have any time to see you today!" I
revelled in my little speech, even though I knew that
Herbert didn't believe one word of it. At that moment,
one of my shoes landed with a terrific splash in the
wash basin, turning my pyjama trousers into wet sacks,

and Herbert advanced on me. ". . . And if you don't marry Helga quickly, you're the biggest clod that I have ever met!" I shouted as we collapsed in a heap on my bed.

8

Jupp's "Birthday"

BY 10.00 hours I was ready to climb into the Komet.
Albert, who was in charge of the ground staff, helped
me into my parachute, and held the small ladder steady
while I climbed into the cockpit. Pitz, it transpired, had
not flown this bird at all, but he told me that he had
seen a test run of its engine and it had sung as sweetly
as a bird. Albert finished adjusting my harness and
reported the aircraft ready for take-off, then Pitz climbed
up the ladder to give me what he referred to as a "last
oiling".

"Everything understood, Mano? Now hold the stick
steady and keep your eyes glued to the pressure
indicator. If there's not enough pressure then pull the
throttle lever back immediately and let her roll out on
the field. If she begins to roll over the perimeter, then
jump for it! Otherwise keep the stick steady, and don't
push her immediately after you're airborne. Drop your
wheels between five and ten metres off the ground—
don't forget! Let the speed pick up to about eight
hundred kilometres an hour beyond the airfield boundary and then pull back steadily on the stick. Don't ease
off. Let her climb until the rocket fades out on you. All
clear? Any questions?"

"All clear, Pitz."

Pitz closed the canopy and I locked it from inside.
From behind the starter truck, Albert gave me the
"thumbs up"—he was ready. I pressed the turbine starter
button—a split second and I could hear the turbine
picking up speed. A gentle whirring sound became a
howl which grew louder and louder. White steam flowed
around the cockpit, and then there was a momentary
silence. For one dreadful moment Fear joined me in
the cockpit and then was gone. The turbine howled
twice more, and I pushed the thrust lever to "idling".
There was a sharp crack as the fuel ignited, and the
pressure gauges jumped. Now! I pushed the thrust
lever to "full thrust", and the pressure gauges jumped
from five to nearly twenty-four atü. It flashed through
my mind that I was fortunate as some of the rocket
motors did not go much over twenty-one atü.

The wheels jumped the blocks and I was rolling.
The rocket motor must have been making an infernal
din but I could hear little more in the cockpit than a
furious rustling sound. My four-ton "bird" rapidly gained
speed, and my eyes were glued to the pressure gauges,
but they didn't budge from the twenty-four atü mark.
For a fraction of a second the needle flicked back to
twenty-two atü, but to my infinite relief it regained its
original point on the dial. The speedometer was now
showing two hundred kilometres per hour but my Komet
was still adhering firmly to the ground. I had forgotten
that the world consisted of anything other than my
fire-spitting mount, the runway stretching ahead of me
and those flickering dials on the instrument panel. The
speedometer was now touching three hundred kilometres
per hour and I could feel that the Messerschmitt was
lighter as though anxious to gain its element, the air.
The madly racing wheels were now hardly touching the
runway, and, then, airborne!

At a height of six or seven metres I pressed the
lever that retracted the landing skid and, simultaneously,
jettisoned the twin-wheeled dolly. Rid of this encum-
brance, the Komet surged forward suddenly, pressing
me back violently into the seat, and at the same time
there was heavy pressure on the control column. Auto-

matically my hand grabbed for the trim wheel for now I had to change the trim setting to two or three degrees nose heavy. For take-off the Komet was trimmed tail heavy—three degrees up to 6,600 pounds and six degrees over this weight—but once in the air the trim had to be reversed immediately for nobody could hold a tail-heavy Komet in a straight climb at speeds around the eight hundred kilometre mark!

In a flash I was fifty metres above Zwischenahn with the speedometer quivering around the seven-hundred and fifty kilometre mark. I gently eased back on the stick, and the aircraft shot upwards—higher and higher, as straight as a bullet into the radiantly blue sky. I throttled back very slightly and began to relax. At that moment a voice crackled in my headphones: "From Bluebell to Bat. Where are the waggon racks?"

Heavens, I had completely forgotten! "Bluebell" was our ground-control station to which I was supposed to report my altitude every thousand metres! I glanced at my altimeter and found that I was already nearing four thousand five hundred metres! I stammered my report:

"From Bat to Bluebell. I am already four-five . . . now five!"

The controller came back: "From Bluebell to Bat—Dozey!"

My rocket-driven elevator thrust me farther and farther into the sky, and now I gave my altitude reports to the controller "according to regulations" at every thousand metres. And then came the moment when the rocket breathed her last, and by the time we had reached eight thousand five hundred metres safe and sound. As the motor cut the Komet seemed to brake hard in mid-air, and I was pushed forward against my harness.

"From Bat to Bluebell. Rocket's cut!" By the time I had released the transmitting button, the impetus had carried my Komet to more than ten thousand metres altitude, and I began to level off. Only a few months before I had believed all that bilge about rocket flying that the average pilot of orthodox aircraft had heard whispered in his mess. It was said that the rocket pilot was strapped in so tight that he could barely breathe; that at take-off the poor fellow's back was pressed so hard against the seat that he had difficulty in maintaining consciousness; that when the rocket cut, the pilot was jerked forward so violently that the harness left bloody weals on his body! Now I knew that all this was complete nonsense. In fact, when the rocket functioned smoothly it gave the "jockey" an indescribably delightful flight.

I put the nose down slightly to gain speed but I was at such a great altitude that I seemed to be detached from Mother Earth. The tiny fields far below and the dots of houses appeared totally unreal. In the distance I could see the haze that was Bremen, and beyond that the silvery blue rim of the Atlantic coast. There was no sign of Zwischenahn or the lake! What if I could not find the airfield again? I began to get a little nervous and began a concentrated search of the terrain below. To my intense relief, I finally spotted the field far below and to starboard. It was all so beautiful and so exhilarating, but then a thought struck me: Wörndl must also have been feeling as gay as this as, unknowingly, he glided back to infinity. I tightened my grip on the stick and began to consider my landing procedure, although I was still some four thousand metres above the ground. It was silly of me, of course. I had still plenty of gliding time in hand.

The serious part of my landing approach did not begin until I was down to fifteen hundred metres. I kept her steady over the forest, gradually sinking to about a thousand metres—crossed the airfield, turning carefully over the eastern edge of the lake—back across the field—altitude seven ... six ... five hundred metres—turning in for the last time—landing cross dead ahead. I was down to three hundred metres, let down the landing skid followed by the flaps. A little too high ... steady ... two-fifty kilometres per hour on the dial ... too fast. Right! The Komet seemed to go down like a bag of stones, but I was still too high. The landing cross sailed past, and then, klunk! With a mighty jerk on my harness I was on the ground, and scraping and jolting across the field, gradually slowing down until, finally, down went the starboard wing and the aircraft came to a standstill. I'd made it! I ripped the oxygen mask from my face, raised my goggles, released the parachute and harness belts, pressed the cockpit canopy upwards and clambered out.

The servicing lorry with Pitz, Herbert and Fritz, and several of the others aboard was already heading in my direction, and to Pitz's unspoken question, I replied: "It was superb, Pitz! I should be glad to climb aboard another Komet and do it all again!"

"Too bad," said Fritz, "I had already reserved your dessert for myself! It's biscuits with chocolate sauce!"

Next day Jupp Mülstroh was to make his third or fourth "sharp" start, and none of us present was ever likely to forget his performance! Jupp was our "court jester"; a highly amusing and unusual character in many ways. Born and bred in Cologne, he was one of those enviable fellows that one meets on rare occasions who stumble through life like clumsy young colts but who invariably land squarely on their feet. Jupp was the complete fatalist. He could never be offended by anything and never offended anybody. He did everything that was demanded of him and, without really intending to be so, was as zealous on duty as at the mess table. He was a constant source of amusing stories, attracted the most absurd happenings, and was a good pilot to boot!

Only a few days before, Jupp, returning to the airfield on the local train after an evening in Oldenburg, happened to stick his head out of the compartment window whereupon the wind promptly blew his cap away into the darkness. Knowing that he would probably be picked up by the military police upon arrival at Bad Zwischenahn for being improperly dressed, he pulled the communication cord and brought the train to a grinding halt. He strolled back along the line, found his cap, and then climbed back into his compartment. By this time, an irate guard had ascertained which compartment was responsible for this cardinal sin, and, finding only Jupp there, demanded an explanation. Jupp finally convinced the guard that his train rocked so badly that his, Jupp's, cap had been jerked from his hand and that rather than report the matter to the State Railways and perhaps get the guard into trouble, quite apart from the fireman and the engineer, he felt that it would be preferable to stop the train! Jupp accepted the guard's deepest apologies with good grace! That was our Jupp!

On the day that Jupp's "sharp" take-off was to be made, the weather left much to be desired. Visibility was not at all good, but it was not bad enough to stop routine flying. And so Jupp took-off with rocket blasting fully, and shot through a gaping hole between two towering cloud banks, and disappeared. A minute passed, and then we heard Jupp's voice over the R/T: "Hey, I can't see a damned thing! Where the hell is the field?" He gave his altitude, and then: "Man alive! I've never made a blind flight in my life! I can't see a damned thing!"

The controller instructed him to reduce his altitude gradually in wide circles until he reached the cloud base, but again Jupp's voice came through the R/T: "Hell, I'm completely lost! Can't see a thing!" Then his radio went dead! Five minutes passed, then six, each of them seeming an eternity. Low-laying clouds had now rolled across the field like a grey blanket from the West, and it had started to drizzle. The visibility was getting steadily worse, and if we had been amused by Jupp's messages a few minutes earlier, our mirth had now completely evaporated and we were thoroughly alarmed. Suddenly, there was a loud hissing noise. Somebody shouted, "Get down! Here comes Jupp!" We flung ourselves on the ground as, like greased lightning, Jupp's Komet shot out of the cloud that was lying virtually in the treetops, and sailed across so close to our heads that we could feel the downwash around our ears. What the hell was Jupp up to? We watched his plane as, somehow, he managed to level off and was now once more haring across the field as though a thousand devils were on his back, pulling up into the cloud over the far boundary. He had still quite a lot of speed left, and as he reappeared it was obvious that he was going to make a wide circuit of the field. He started his final approach but was obviously still going too fast. Somehow he pulled up the Komet, dropped his flaps, and then went into such a frightening sideslip that we instinctively closed our eyes. Surely this was the end! But no, with more luck than skill, he somehow corrected and touched down—just like that! The Komet slithered along the ground with us in pursuit, cheering our heads off.

When we arrived Jupp was standing quietly and with becoming modesty by his aircraft, Toni Thaler was the first to regain his breath: "Hell, Mühlstroh, are you still alive?"

"At your service, Sir!" Jupp replied.

Flabbergasted, Toni could only say: "Well, I never! You've got a bloody sight more luck than sense!"

"My wife says exactly the same thing, Sir!" Jupp answered in his inimitable Cologne dialect—and from the look on his face he might have just accomplished the first landing on Mars.

"Why didn't you come down right away, or stay under the cloud base?"

"Well, you see, Captain, it all happened so quickly that I didn't have time for proper reflection! I was through those clouds almost before I knew that they were there, and when I looked back for the hole through which I had climbed, it had gone! So I just flew around for a while pondering. Then I said to myself, 'Jupp, if you stay up here and worry you'll blow your top.' So, deciding that if I was going to hit anything I should much rather hit it at speed, I put the nose down and aimed the aircraft in the direction that I hoped was that of the field. When I dropped out of that cloud I could see nothing but forest—and then a road. I said to myself, 'Jupp, that's where you went for a walk with your wife the other day, remember?'—and as I was remembering that and thinking what a pleasant walk it had been, there in front of me was the field. So here I am!"

I could see Toni Thaler's face getting redder and redder with his efforts to restrain himself from roaring with laughter, and then he said: "In that case, Mühlstroh, you'll have to invite your wife to a decent birthday* celebration. I think that she deserves it as much as you!"

"Yes, sir!" replied Jupp. "Will it be paid for out of State funds?"

---

*It was the custom in the Luftwaffe to celebrate "a birthday" when somebody managed to survive in one piece when, logically, they should be dead. In other words, they had been "born" again, and that day was their birthday.

9

"Ski Hail"

JUPP'S FUN and games in the clouds over Bad Zwischenahn proved to be the last Komet flight from our field
for some considerable time. It was not merely the
weather, which had steadily deteriorated, snow alternat-
ing with fog, but also a determined effort on the part
of our engineers to solve once and for all this deadly
problem of negative acceleration, and empty "Powered
Egg" airframes stood around in the hangars while the
rocket motors screamed away on every test stand. In
consequence, we pilots started to "gammel", this slang
term being used to describe the ultimate in sheer
frustration; a brief period of pleasant idleness progressing
into a far longer period of deadly tedium.

Unable to fly, we felt much the same as a dedicated
angler might feel faced by a river teeming with fish
when lacking rod and line. We plumbed the depths of
depression. Things got steadily worse. We sat around
the mess talking, and when we had exhausted all topics
of conversation, we would polish up on our languages,
listen to the radio, read, anything to pass the time away.
In fact, we had got to the stage where we were fed up
with seeing each other's faces when, out of the blue,
Herbert Langer, Fritz Kelb and I received an order to
report immediately to Rechlin and collect one ME 163.

But we were not only to collect it but to deliver it also *by air*—towing it behind a Bf 110 all the way from Rechlin to Bad Zwischenahn!

Early the next morning, one of our Bf 110 tow-planes was prepared for our departure, and while Fritz and I checked our flight plan with the ground control centre, Herbert checked with the met. boys. The weather was not at all promising, but we were soon settled in the Bf 110 with Herbert hunched behind the controls, and Fritz and I seated aft. We had been airborne for thirty minutes or so when, all of a sudden, Herbert went into a sharp bank. A thick blanket of cloud was now strewn below us, and as Herbert tightened his turns we could see him peering downwards with a puzzled expression on his face. He levelled off and flew on for a few more minutes, and then started banking again. Neither Fritz nor I had to be told that our Herbert, whose navigation had never been outstanding, had lost his whereabouts some time ago, and he was now trying to spot a railway station or some other landmark through one of the small gaps in the carpet of murky cloud. At last Herbert found his station, and we went straight down on to the deck in a series of sharp turns, and proceeded to beat up the station at low level while Herbert endeavoured to ascertain his position. I heard Fritz's voice in my headphones: "Mano, what wood do you prefer for coffins?"

A shout came from Herbert: "You'd better peel your eyes for the name of that ruddy station double quick, you parasites, or else you are likely to be buried in cigar boxes!"

But somehow he managed on his own, for after a couple more low runs, he pulled up the nose of the Bf 110 and set some sort of course, and, much to our surprise—and probably to Herbert's as well—we landed at Rechlin an hour later.

It was bitterly cold as we, together with a few mechanics, tugged the Me 163 to the starting line, and attached a thin steel cable to the two aircraft. My teeth were chattering and I had difficulty in controlling my shivering despite my flying suit as I settled down be-

hind the Me 163s control column. This is going to be
some winter sport, I thought to myself, and I was to be
proved right. One of the ground crew waved a flag,
and the trusty old Bf 110 started down the runway,
sending up billowing clouds of snow which completely
obscured my view. The Me 163 gradually gained speed
and juddered over some bad patches in the runway. I
kept the aircraft on the ground as long as I dared to
ensure that she did not stall or get over the airscrew
backwash of the tug. Then, with a jerk, I was airborne
and above the swirling snow. There was our Bf 110 in
front of me, with Fritz gesticulating wildly from the
rear seat! He ended his performance by crossing his
arms over his head and then tapping his forehead with
a finger. It was then that I realized that we had only
cleared some trees on the airfield boundary by a metre
or so! A truly close shave! Evidently Fritz's gesticula-
tions had been intended to convey to me the dim view
he took of Herbert's appallingly bad take-off demonstration. But no! It dawned on me that I was the culprit,
holding the Me 163 on the ground for too long, and I
could imagine the ribbing that I should receive when
we eventually landed at Bad Zwischenahn!

Dragging along behind that cable I got steadily
colder and colder. I jammed the stick between my knees
and thrust both hands under my arm-pits in an attempt
to keep them warm. But it did not help much and,
anyway, I couldn't fly like that. The Me 163 was jinking
about and Fritz was once more gesticulating from the
rear seat of the tow-plane. What hell of a flight! Then I
remembered that somebody had once told me that singing keeps the blood stream circulating and your body
warm, so I started to sing. The circulation of my blood
still seemed to come to a dead standstill before reaching
my fingers and toes, and I became progressively colder
and colder. I would have given a month's rations for a
hot water bottle, and I resolved that I would be clutching just such an item if I was called upon to make any
similar delivery flights. By this time the first houses of
Bad Zwischenahn were swimming into view. I dropped
the cable at about six hundred metres above the field,

saw the Bf 110 bank away sharply to starboard, with Fritz pulling faces at me, and then concentrated on my landing. The wind was just right, so I ignored the landing cross and touched down a few hundred metres away from it, slithering almost to the doors of the big hangar.

The personnel entry door in the hangar flew open and Toni Thaler came dashing towards me. I was still trying to ease my stiff and near frozen legs from the cockpit when he began thoroughly tearing me off a strip! This was not a bit like Toni, and I was speechless with amazement at his performance. After all, there was no flying going on around the field and my landing had been "clean", merely a few hundred metres away from where it should have been! Hell, I had spared our mechanics and the towing vehicle quite a lot of work by planting the aircraft on their doorstep. But Toni was bellowing at me as though I was a cat that had just planted something unpleasant on the carpet. Were we not the best of comrades despite those two stars on his shoulders? Perhaps he had just had a row with his wife.

"Toni, help me get these damned boots off. My feet have just about had it!" I said, ignoring his apparent fury. That was the last straw! Toni now really stood on his rank, telling me to snap to attention and that he would report me for insubordination! He then began to bestow on me such endearing epithets as "boy pilot" and "joystick suckling", and it began to dawn on me that this was no joke! I came to attention and, with the most arrogant expression I could muster, said: "I would respectfully mention, Captain—Sir, that I have made as many landings in the Me 163 as the Captain has himself!"

It was as though I had kicked him in the teeth. "We will discuss this on another occasion"—he roared, and stamped off in the direction of the administrative block. Unfortunately, we never reverted to our former relationship for he never forgave me, and from that moment Toni spoke to me only when he had to give me a direct order.

There was still no sign of any flying from Bad

Zwischenahn, and our inactivity became increasingly
unbearable. The tedium was broken for a few days
when we Komet pilots were given orders to evacuate
our quarters at the field and move into billets in the
town. This change in our accommodation was made for
our sake—or rather the sake of our expensive training—
for, as the enemy bomber formations grew in size and
progressively extended their range, the day that they
would attempt to plant as many holes in our field as in
a gruyere cheese could not be far away, whereas Bad
Zwischenahn did not present them with a worth-while
target. As every one of us had nearly a million marks'
worth of training behind him—each "sharp" take-off
with a Komet cost about ten thousand reichsmarks in
fuel alone—it was clear that "our bunch" was now looked
upon as valuable state property, and if we had to lose
our lives the powers-that-be preferred it not to be as a
result of a casual bomb!

Hilda Dyckerhoff now came into her element. As
was to be expected, a number of the daughters of Bad
Zwischenahn had already lost their hearts to some of
our pilots and there had been several quiet engage-
ments around the countryside. Other girls' hearts were
already beating for more of our pilots, and now came
the problem of distributing these eligible young bachelors in a seemly way! This is where Hilda's diplomacy
reached new heights. There were rooms available in
most of the better houses of Bad Zwischenahn, or could
be made available at short notice—meaning, of course,
mainly those houses in which dwelled unmarried daughters! Hilda went to work with tact and decorum, and
the results were anything but those that many expected.
Those houses with eligible daughters found themselves
sheltering lodgers that in no way qualified for their
daughters, while the eligible bachelors found themselves accommodated at some distance from their "centres
of interest". It was not that Hilda was narrow-minded.
On the contrary—but she believed that it was better to
be safe than sorry.

*   *   *

And so the days passed until, one day, somebody shouted, "Ski hail!" Before actually starting training on the Me 163 all those months back, the whole of Test-Commando 16 had been sent to the Zugspitze for four weeks, the idea being that the high altitude of this delightful place would acclimatize us for flight at extreme altitudes as well as, if not better than, the unpleasant pressure chamber. The skiing that we enjoyed during those blissful days on the Zugspitze would always remain as one of our fondest memories, and that shout of "Ski hail" set several of us thinking. What was the sense in sitting around on our posteriors here in Bad Zwischenahn when we could be enjoying ourselves and improving our altitude fitness on the Zugspitze! The idea was there, but how could we "bring it home" to the chief?

Straight away we initiated a whispering campaign based on the theory that a dripping tap will wear away the hardest stone, and our first "action" did not take place until breakfast one beautiful morning early in March. As on every other morning, Major Späte strode into the mess and greeted us with his usual "Hail, Comrades!" On this particular morning our reply was unusual indeed, a thundering "Ski hail, Sir!"

Späte was one of those people with the ability to suppress any sign of surprise, and our unusual greeting produced no reaction whatsoever. But we ensured the continual "dripping of the water", and finally the evening came when Späte, sitting with a group of us around one of the most expensive bottles of wine from Helmut Dyckerhoff's seemingly inexhaustible cellar, gave me a sarcastic grin, and said: "All right, Ziegler. You can arrange quarters for twelve or fourteen men in some place over two thousand metres in altitude, and you can leave with the first transport the day after tomorrow!"

The problem now was to *find* accommodation. I already knew that there was no accommodation at Schneefernerhouse on the Zugspitze, and then I suddenly thought of the spot where I had spent my honeymoon. All my friends had thought me mad when I had decided to spend the first weeks of my marriage in the Sellajoch-House, two thousand two hundred me-

tres up in the Dolomites. As soon as Späte left, I grabbed
the telephone and asked the sleepy operator to connect
me with the local military commander's residence in
Brixen in the South Tyrol. I had my connection in
seven minutes—something of a record in telephonic
communications in those days! My call must have awak-
ened a sleepy orderly, and it took all my persuasion to
get him to rouse the duty officer. Quite understandably,
the duty officer was not exactly friendly, but as soon as
I started using terms like "Special Commando" and
"Rocket Pilots", and insinuated that I was calling at the
behest of the General of Fighter Aviation, I had him
figuratively grovelling on his knees, and he assured me
that quarters would be arranged immediately!

I feel sure that Späte believed the task of arranging
such accommodation at short notice would be as difficult as acquiring overnight a cigar stub from Winston
Churchill's ashtray, and I am equally sure that the
expression on my face when I reported my success to
him at eight o'clock the next morning must have revealed my malicious pleasure. But he didn't bat an
eyelid, merely signing my travel orders which instructed
me to leave on the following day to ensure that billets
were available for my comrades.

Feeling very satisfied with myself, I left for Brixen,
but between Oldenburg and Hanover I discovered to
my consternation that I had been counting my chickens
before they were hatched. My travel documents were
examined by the usual railway military police who
promptly informed me that Brixen had become a part
of "Operational Area Alp-Foreland" and, therefore, a
prohibited area to all military personnel not concerned
with the defence of the area. The best laid schemes . . . !
The M.P. advised me to return to Bad Zwischenahn
and shrugged his shoulders unconcernedly when I told
him that I could not return without completing my
task.

"As far as I am concerned, you can do whatever
you prefer. I was merely endeavouring to save you a
wasted journey to Munich. They will only send you
back here anyway!"

What now? It did not seem that I had much to lose, so I travelled on to Munich, carefully preparing and rehearsing the story that I proposed telling the chief R.T.O. My frame of mind was most definitely "do or die" by the time the train reached Munich. I marched purposefully into the station R.T.O. office and slid my orders across the desk to the duty N.C.O. He merely glanced at them, passed them back to me, and said: "Aren't you lucky, sir! The entry restrictions on this area have just been rescinded!"

Early that evening I was confronted by another duty N.C.O., but this time in the District Commanding Officer's official residence in Brixen. With a beaming smile on his face, he reported that everything was in order and that our billets had been arranged in St. Ulrich. For a moment I could hardly believe my ears. The altitude of St. Ulrich was hardly a thousand metres and totally useless for high-altitude acclimatization!

"It is absolutely essential that we get to Sellajoch!" I shouted, and demanded a telephone connection with Sellajoch-House immediately. My luck was in, for the landlord, Valentini, remembered me from prewar days. He told me that his guest house was empty but, unfortunately, under attachment orders from the High Commissioner for the Alp-Foreland military district. As this high dignitary had his residence in Bolzen, it appeared that I should have to proceed there the next day to plead my cause. My interview the next morning was short and to the point. I just about convinced the good officer that there was no chance of final victory for Germany without our Test-Commando, and that Sellajoch-House was absolutely essential for our training! Ten minutes later I was sending a telegram to Bad Zwischenahn informing the chief that all arrangements had been made!

There was only one snag. There was not a trace of snow to be seen! Not even on the walls of Langkofel. Warm breezes and spring flowers, yes, but no snow, and we wanted ski-ing! When the train arrived the next evening with the lucky "altitude candidates", instead of receiving deep and profound thanks, I was threatened

with dismemberment on the spot! "We have not travelled two days just to pick flowers!" they said, but after
a superb supper the paucity of snow was temporarily
forgotten. Then another problem faced us. One of the
boys wanted to buy some cigarettes but none of us had
any Italian lire, and here the German reichsmark was
as valueless as a used cinema ticket! However, the solution of this one had to await the morning, and took the
shape of a kindly paymaster who let us have a thousand
cigarettes for reichsmarks. Cigarettes were, by that time,
one of the rarest of commodities, their rarity being
comparable only with that of alcohol in any form.

It was already late in the afternoon when what
must have been just about the slowest train in Europe
carried us through the Grödner Valley to Plan, and,
wonder of wonders, the first snow! It got thicker and
thicker as we made our late-night climb to Sellajoch,
and when Valentini, that angel with the Italian accent,
received us with a midnight meal of spicey bean soup,
man-sized cutlets, fried potatoes and salad, my reputa-
tion had been saved!

Next morning, after an excellent breakfast, we took
stock of our resources. We still lacked lire, and we were
short of six pairs of skis. More in hopes than expectations,
I strapped on my skis, and together with Langer, Glogner
and Mühlstroh on a sledge, made my way down to
Wolkenstein to look up the paymaster residing there.
We needed the equivalent of two thousand reichsmarks,
an amount that called for a set of logarithms to convert
into lire. Officially, of course, we had no right to ask
for this money. I cannot say what the chief had in mind
regarding finance when he sanctioned the expedition,
but we were to enjoy absolutely incredible luck—all
paymasters in the Alp-Foreland area must have been
recruited from a host of angels. Not only did this gentleman in Wolkenstein provide us with the money in the
friendliest possible way; he offered us six pairs of skis
from a selection in his own cellar!

Cheerfully, we made our way back to Sellajoch-
House. On the way down we had left Jupp Mühlstroh
at a guest house in Plan la Gralba, and we could hardly

believe our eyes when we returned to collect him. There
was our Jupp, reclining at his ease, sipping red wine,
and enjoying the company of a curvaceous, raven-haired
beauty! When we had more or less recovered from our
shock, Jupp, who an hour before had not spoken a
word of Italian, introduced us: "Olga—grand amore!"

Officially named the Albergo Plan de Gralba, this
guest house was ever after known to us as the "Albergo
Mühlstroh"!

During our stay in Sellajoch our daily routine consisted entirely of eating, sleeping and, of course, ski-
ing. The ski-ing was organized by three "instructors"—
Kelb, Schametz and myself, all of us having been
brought up among mountains and almost born on skis.
Those were indescribably beautiful hours we spent on
the broad snowdrifts between Langkofel, Sellatürmen
and distant Marmolate. Each sundown we stool in silent
admiration, marvelling as the enormous cliffs changed
their colours from deep brown to fiery red, while the
snow beneath these rocky monsters turned dark blue
and the sky from turquoise to green. Day after day we
were convulsed with laughter, such as when our fearless "rocketeer" Oeltjen became thoroughly confused
and landed flat on his face several times, or when Nelte
became hopelessly entangled with his skis and was unable to extricate himself without help.

Then, one day, a message was sent to the Sellajoch-
House to tell us that a feast was being held in the valley
and that this was to be followed by a dance. "That's for
us!" shouted Fritz Kelb, and off he went with several of
the others. Together with Herbert, I stayed in the guest
house as we planned on making the Sella-Tour the
next morning and a good night's sleep was essential.
But our night's sleep was to be far from good! At about
4 a.m. I was shaken awake by Fritz.

"Mano, get up. Mühlstroh's missing!"

For a moment I couldn't imagine what the hell he
was talking about, and then, gathering my wits slowly, I
said: "What happened?"

"Mülhstroh's gone! Disappeared in a fog on the

way up! We've been waiting an hour already, but there is no sign of him!"

I was wide awake by this time. "You're not joking, Fritz, are you?"

"Hell, no! I don't feel much like joking at the moment! Jupp took off his skis on the way—he had a broken strap—and was following right behind us. Then came a bit of snow and fog . . . and he was gone!"

"He was probably sloshed again," I answered furiously as I struggled into my trousers. Lost in the mountains at this time of the morning! I laced up my ski boots. "Come on. We must find the bloody fool before he freezes to death!"

"Schametz has already gone to look for him," said Fritz, "but he's not back either!" Then we were racing down the wooden steps. There was no time to lose! Within a matter of seconds we had strapped on our skis and were heading in the direction of Plan. The tracks made by Fritz's party were already, for the most part, covered by freshly-fallen snow and levelled by the mountain winds, and there were some dark, forbidding clouds rolling across the night sky. The moon was visible for only a few minutes at a time, illuminating the dull brown cliffs with silvery granite patches. We stopped at intervals, shouting Jupp's name, but there was no sound or sign of him. Ten minutes later we met Schametz coming up. He told us that he had gone all the way down to Plan and, to be on the safe side, had called in at the "Albergo Mühlstroh" as well, but there was no trace of Jupp!

"Where did you see him last?" I asked. Schametz pointed to a bend in the road higher up. "Just about there. He took off his skis at that point," he said.

"All right then. We'll split up now and start back along the track, searching on both sides. And if we don't find him we will have to wake up the whole guest house and continue the search with torches!"

We had only gone a few metres when there was a shout from Schametz who had been searching on our right. "Hey, come over here!" He pointed to a hole that could have been made by somebody falling down in the snow. There was a barely visible track stretching away from the hole towards the mist-shrouded field. We followed like bloodhounds, and five minutes later we were standing by the remains of a ruined cow-man's hut. Our search was over. Stretched out full length on the floor next to an iron stove was the unconscious body of Jupp Mühlstroh, a box of matches still gripped between the cold fingers. The battered door stood wide open, and an icy cold wind was howling through holes in the walls. I felt as though I could beat the living daylights out of our idiot from Cologne. That we had found him at all was a miracle. The little iron stove had long since lost its chimney pipe and was stuffed to bursting point with dry straw. A large pile of hay was packed right behind the stove, and next to Jupp's hand were a dozen half-burned matches. Had he succeeded in lighting the stove, the whole hut would have gone up like tinder, and he would have had no chance to escape! On the other hand, if we had not found him when we had, he would have frozen to death within an hour or two!

We carried him back to the guest-house where we gave him the full treatment. We rubbed Jupp mercilessly with snow until he started to groan. His eyes flickered open, then he muttered weakly: "Bloody hell! Have I got a hangover!"

The next afternoon as Herbert and I entered the forecourt of the guesthouse after our Sella-Tour, an apparition met our startled eyes. It was none other than our Fritz, but a *different* Fritz! Unlike the normal, untidy Fritz that we had come to know so well, this Fritz was immaculate! His jacket had been pressed, his trousers sported knife-edge creases, he was wearing a freshly laundered shirt, and he had had the closest shave that had left his face as pink as a baby's! With a happy smile on his face, Fritz let us into his secret: he had a rendezvous with "Olga, grande amore!"

"Now that's what I call silly," I said. "Imagine going down there on a fool's errand and then having to spend two hours toiling back up the mountain at midnight!"

"Mano, you don't understand!" Fritz waved his hand deprecatingly. "I shall be doing that climb tomorrow morning!" And off he went towards his assignation.

We had an agreement that anyone of us who enjoyed a "successful" rendezvous contributed ten lire to the "table fund". This "table fund" was our invention, and was kept going by contributions made as a result of crude mistakes during ski-ing lessons, slovenly table manners, and other misdemeanours—and, of course, shafts from Cupid's bow! It was quite late when we finally turned in that night. Everybody was in a festive mood, and we had a good sing-song, while good old Valentini dug out a couple of bottles of Asti spumante. When at last we said "goodnight" to each other, it was long past midnight, and there were more than a few smiles at the sight of Fritz's empty bed.

Fritz was back for his breakfast exactly at 09.00 hours, and only waved his hand as we greeted him with loud shouts of "Bravo!" I pushed the "table fund" box towards him, and we all waited eagerly to see the colour of our Casanova's money. But Fritz merely made a tired gesture: "Comrades, I've spared myself ten lire!"

Never again did Fritz look so immaculate as before his abortive rendezvous!

Two days after Fritz's sad loss of prestige, we were all ski-ing down the steep Langkofel Gap which took us straight back to the Sellajoch House. As we took the final vault there, in front of our unbelieving eyes, was the chief! Yes, Wolfgang Späte in person!

It appeared that the good doctor had insisted that he have some sick leave as he had still not recovered entirely from his accident, so he had decided to join us. He was not allowed to ski so he spent his days sunbathing and modelling in snow. His skilled hands created a larger-than-life reclining Aphrodite which graced the forecourt of the guest-house. We soon christened this delightful snow maiden "Mrs. Kelb" which, of course, annoyed our Fritz intensely. It is true that her form lost some of its charms after each sunny day, but she was carefully restored each evening, and Späte really surpassed himself in the care that he lavished on his cre-

ation for the two weeks of his leave plus the eight
additional days that he managed to wangle.

All too soon the time came for our departure from
Sellajoch. I stood talking to our host and, among other
things, mentioned the sorry state of the bar at our
airfield. As the mess officer, I knew only too well that
our "cupboards" were virtually bare, and we could hardly
drink T-stoff! Valentini then surprised me by suggesting that a friend of a friend of his could perhaps
organize eighty litres of plum brandy in exchange for
three kilos of saccharine. This was wartime barter at its
best, and I agreed at once. Valentini gave me the address in Bolzen where I was supposed to collect the
beverage, and I could send the saccharine with the next
party of ski-ing "rocketeers". Fair enough! That evening we had an official "duty hour" for letter writing,
and each one of us wrote to our parents, wife, fiancée,
friends—the subject—please send immediately every
available box of saccharine tablets to Lieutenant Ziegler,
c/o Test-Commando 16!

After the others had gone to bed, Späte, Langer
and I stayed up awhile to talk. The chief ordered a
bottle of expensive wine, filled our glasses, and then
said: "Now listen to me carefully, and keep this to
yourselves. Understand?" Upon receiving our nods, he
continued: "I must leave for the Eastern Front and take
over a Messerschmitt 109 wing there. Thaler is to be
my successor and will command the Test-Commando,
while Pitz will take over on the training side!"

We could hardly believe our ears. If the summit of
the Langkofel had rolled down into the valley we could
hardly have evinced more surprise. Herbert, who had
known Späte longer than any of us, and was on the
most familiar terms with him, made an incredulous
face, and said: "But this *can't* be true, Major! It is
impossible! Now that we are nearly ready and will shortly
be forming the first operational squadrons, you are to
leave us? Impossible!"

"And yet it is true," Späte replied calmly, "and
nothing can be done about it! In a month or two I shall
be away. The orders from above have arrived already!"

Me 109G

We simply could not imagine our Test-Commando without Späte. We knew only too well the shortcomings that still had to be ironed out of our Komet, and that it would be more important than ever that, in the months ahead, we would have someone like Späte standing by us. After all, he had flown the Me 163 from the very beginning. Thaler could not possibly replace him! He had not flown the Komet for many months, and consequently he knew less about it than we did ourselves! On the other hand, Pitz was a superb pilot through and through, but never the leader of such a Commando. Perhaps there was something else behind this transfer. In fact, we felt sure there must be. The news could not have been worse. Whatever the reason for this transfer, it bode only ill for the future of our Commando and ourselves!

10

Tragedy at Rechlin

A SPECIAL task awaited us immediately after our return to Bad Zwischenahn. There was to be a demonstration and comparison-flying between the latest combat aircraft at the Rechlin Experimental Centre, and among the spectators would be Hermann Goering himself! Naturally, the Komet would be among the latest aircraft types to be demonstrated, and it was impressed upon us that it was of the utmost importance that the demonstration be as impressive as possible as it would have far-reaching consequences on the further development of the Me 163 and also on the production priority allocated to the fighter. If successful, the demonstration could be of infinite assistance to the higher command of the Luftwaffe.

As Heini Dittmar was still out of the running, his recovery in hospital from injuries received in a crash at Peenemünde late in 1942 having been protracted, there was only one pilot who we could be sure would give a suitably impressive demonstration—Pitz! It was always possible that the rocket motor would pack up slap over the heads of the Luftwaffe dignitaries, and of *that* happened only Pitz could be relied upon to pull the fat out of the fire. Of course, even Pitz could not do anything if the rocket gave up the ghost at low altitude and low speed, but if he was high enough he could always demonstrate his "accelerated low-level flying", forcing his aircraft down on to the deck as only he knew how, and foxing the spectators into believing that the motor had been cut intentionally! On the other hand, if the demonstration flight went wrong, there were plenty of people who were opposed to the Me 163 who would take advantage of the situation to press for the discontinuation of further development.

Rechlin was known the world over. Not only was it the arena for flight-testing an infinite variety of weapons that had been developed in the utmost secrecy. It was also the airfield where aircraft were put through their paces by the top German test pilots before being passed to service units. The last bugs had been wrung from well-known types here, and a parachute played as much a part of Rechlin life as a milk pail in a cowshed. These tests were made under the constantly critical eyes of the leading Luftwaffe officers while, quite frequently, there were high-ranking visitors from the air arms of our allied countries.

On the day of the vital demonstration, not only were Goering and his retinue present, but also high-ranking Italian and Japanese officers. Aircraft after aircraft taxied out to take-off, were given full throttle by their respective pilots, and roared off down the runway. Once airborne, they were demonstrated in low-level flight like so many mannequins, cavorted above the field, tickled the nerves of the spectators with a few low-level mock attacks, and then screamed past in fast runs "on the deck" before pulling steeply up into a series of rolls over the perimeter and then landing. Their pilots appeared to handle them with all the knowledge and carelessness of an intimate relationship.

The mechanics finally began their last pre-flight checks on Pitz's Komet, and a few moments after an Me 262 jet fighter had landed, Pitz climbed into his cockpit, started the turbine and, within seconds, had raced down the runway with a deafening roar, dropped his wheels, and rocketed almost vertically into the sky, leaving a

Me 262

vivid flaming trail. All spectators had their eyes glued
to the rapidly disappearing Komet, while the others—
those who had never seen a Komet before—were rooted
to the spot with their mouths agape! Pitz gave a really
spectacular show. At four thousand metres he throttled
back to "first stage" thrust, did a half-loop and came
out in inverted flight, and then rolled skilfully to avoid
negative acceleration. He then put his Komet into a
fantastic dive aimed straight at the stand occupied by
Goering and his guests. The Komet whistled down like
a falling meteor, lower and lower, until, at about a
hundred metres from the ground, Pitz rammed the
throttle lever forward to "third stage" or full power,
and raced across the VIP stand barely ten metres above
their heads! The noise was appalling. Hermann ducked,
the colour drained from the faces of the Italians, and
even the stoical Japanese lost their inscrutable smiles
for a moment. But Pitz was already far away, and at
between five and six thousand metres a slight thump
announced the end of his fuel.

The Reichsmarshal was now following Pitz's beautiful spirals with his binoculars. Pitz put the nose of his Komet down to gain more speed, and then executed a few elegant aerobatic figures and, finally, at about two thousand metres, he began diving towards the airfield once more, whistled across the runway, pulled up and then turned in calmly to make his final approach. It was then that something incomprehensible happened! While Pitz was gliding in towards the airfield, an Me 262, which had taken off before the Komet, turned in for a landing approach as well, coming from the starboard quarter, and thus cutting right in front of Pitz's aircraft! Pitz could not go round again without rocket power, and he was now forced to make an evasive turn to avoid colliding with the other aircraft. There was enough space to avoid the Me 262, but Pitz's landing glide now carried him away over that part of the field where soft sand supplanted the grass! We all knew that only a miracle could help Pitz then, for he could do absolutely nothing to avoid landing on the sand. And then it happened! The Komet touched down, tilted forward right away because of the tremendous braking effect of the soft sand, and Pitz appeared to pull back on his stick, his landing skid momentarily leaving the sand for a short hop before crashing down again. The Komet skidded forward for twenty or thirty metres and, for a moment, we thought that the danger was over. Then, all at once, the aircraft jerked to a stop and the tail swung over like a halberd! The Komet had turned over on its back and lay there, steaming and hissing from every panel ... and Pitz was under it! Horror rooted us to the spot for a second, and then we were racing for the nearest lorry. Every second counted now! The fire tender was already haring across the field at full speed, and we followed in the lorry. The explosion could come at any moment, and, if it did, well ... it would be of little use looking for our Pitz! Thunder and lightning! Was one of the most beautiful performances ever given in a Komet to end like this? And Pitz of all people!

"Faster, man, faster!" I screamed at our driver,

noticing only at that moment that it was an unknown *major* gripping the steering wheel. He did not say a word, but I could see that his foot was hard down on the accelerator. We arrived on the scene only seconds after the fire tender which was already spraying the aircraft with jets of water. We grabbed the Komet and heaved it over, without a thought that we could all be blown to Hades any moment. We ripped off the half-open canopy and pulled Pitz from his seat. Only just conscious, he was obviously in a bad way. Pints of T-stoff must have flowed over his back while he was trapped in the overturned aircraft, from his combination smock was hanging from his back in damp, charred tatters, and the skin on his back had become a jelly-like mass in places. He made an effort to smile at us. "Take it easy, Pitz! They will look after you," we said, but our hearts were heavy.

We returned to Bad Zwischenahn late the same afternoon. "Maybe they will break up the Commando altogether now," Fritz muttered as we sat that evening over a glass that had failed to cheer. Yes, it seemed

Fw 190

possible that they might do just that! After all, what
had we achieved in our six months' existence? From the
thirty pilots that had been ordered to Bad Zwischenahn
in the autumn, several were already dead and others—
the most important ones—were badly injured. No, it
could not go on like this for much longer, and then
what would happen to us? Back again to Bf 109s and
Fw 190s? Crawling around at what by now seemed to
us a snail's pace and taking a half-hour to get "upstairs"?
No, surely not. We were wedded to the Komet, devil's
sledge though it may be!

11

The First Komet Squadrons

OUR SOJOURN at Sellajoch soon appeared to have been the calm before the storm, for Späte arrived back at the field from Berlin with a sackful of new orders. Three days later a trio of harmless-looking civilians turned up on our airfield and we were given orders to teach them to fly the Komet—but double quick! At that time all civilians looked pretty harmless to us, and objects of a combination of envy and pity, but these three, whose names were Voy, Perschall and Lamm, were particularly deserving of the latter—they were to be "acceptance" pilots for production Komets! We sympathized with them—we tried our best to keep them cheerful but we believed that they had bought themselves one-way express tickets for the graveyard!

Both our captains—Böhner and Olejnik—received orders at this time to proceed to Venlo and Wittmundhafen respectively to begin preparations for the formation of the first two operational Komet squadrons. Special advance detachments had already been installed at both airfields, preparing the runways and workshops, and it transpired that Karl Voy was supposed to test the Me 163Bs at Wittmundhafen as they were delivered from the factories, as Messerschmitt's field at Lechfeld

was no longer suitable for production flight testing—
the enemy's bombers had seen to that!

The General of Fighters was also pressing hard to
get our rocket fighters into action. We had been told
that we had to get the Komet to a state of operational
readiness just as rapidly as was humanly possible, and
every order was now stamped "Urgent".

During a confidential talk with a group of us, Späte
explained the rocket fighter "defence plan" as it was
envisaged at that time. In short, the idea was to have a
chain of Me 163B bases stretching from the north to
the extreme south of Germany. This "rocket fighter
chain" would soon put a stop to all enemy daylight
penetrations—or, at least, so it was hoped. In theory,
this plan was perfect. Our Komet's range was only
about eighty kilometres, and so the bases would be
situated approximately one hundred and fifty kilometres
apart, and there was little doubt that, given enough
operational units of Komets on these bases, the plan
had a good chance of success. There were unlikely to
be any difficulties regarding the quantity of production
of the Komet, for its airframe and the rocket motor
were simple to produce; but it was another matter
when it came to the pilots to man these aircraft! It was
a complete puzzle to us as to how they were going to
find several hundred rocket fighter pilots required to
fulfil such a plan! They could not be plucked from
trees like fruit!

Nevertheless, we went to work with renewed vigour.
The rocket motors, which, in the meantime, had been
tested and tested again by Eli and Otto and their crews,
now gave a good account of themselves—at least, they
did not explode so frequently. But to make up for this
increased reliability, they now stank so dreadfully at
altitude that the tears poured down the cheeks of us
pilots. Inside the cockpit it was as though one had been
chopping onions for the whole Wing! The fantastic
odour was not dangerous in itself, but the poor pilot
felt much as the conductor of a symphony orchestra
would feel if he knew that a sneezing attack was about
to descend on him slap in the middle of a concert! It

was extremely disconcerting, and the knowledge that it was caused by a minute leakage of T-stoff through a gasket gave us the uncomfortable feeling of sitting in an open gunpowder barrel with a lighted cigarette between our teeth.

In spite of everything, our three civilians passed out on the Komet with flying colours in only three weeks, and we gave them a wonderful send-off, the more hectic portion of the evening being followed by the "confirmation" ceremony with Späte's "loco oilcan".

Now this "loco oilcan" calls for some explanation. I cannot say if it had been Späte's own idea or one that he had borrowed, but I well remember the day that he appointed me mess officer and ordered me to get hold of one of those "loco oilcans" immediately! I set off with only the vaguest idea of what I had been sent to acquire, and after drawing a blank at several hardware stores in Bad Zwischenahn and Oldenburg, I happened to be passing a large locomotive shed. And then it dawned on me what Späte wanted—one of those oilcans that looked something like an elongated Aladdin's Lamp. Standing in the doorway of the shed, I watched a portly old boy covered almost from head to toe in soot and grease, applying just such an oilcan to an ancient and decrepit locomotive. He pressed a protruding, finger-length button and the can immediately ejected a very respectable stream of thick, black oil from the end of the long and pointed spout. Plucking up my courage, I asked the old maintenance man if he would sell the oilcan to me, but his reaction was very unfavourable. It was obviously only my uniform that prevented him from expressing himself in the most forcible terms as to what he thought of my insult. The oilcan was his badge of office; it was as much a part of him as his greasy old cap which must have been barely a half-score years younger than himself. But there was no stopping me then. I explained that I was one of the lads from an airfield at Bad Zwischenahn and that the acquisition of just such an oilcan was vital to our war effort.

"In that case, it's quite a different matter," he replied, and handed the can to me there and then, oil and all!

I hurried back to the field, clutching my oilcan, and, together with the senior warrant officer of our ground staff, set about cleaning the thing with paraffin and petrol, and then with pure alcohol. After that we boiled it, and then allowed it to soak in alcohol overnight. The next day I boiled it once more and, that evening, presented it to the chief. I was as proud as if I had taken Moscow single-handed! Späte looked at the battered object upon which I had lavished so much work and affection, smiled, and then proceeded to fill the can with pure Geneve. Telling me to make myself comfortable, to lean back a little and to open my mouth wide, he solemnly aimed the pointed spout carefully at my mouth, and shot three jets of the gin straight down my throat! It was not too bad at all, though it tasted a little of lubricating oil. From that time on, the "loco oilcan" was used as an expression of the highest honour, but when Späte finally left us, I emptied the can, polished it and put it aside. Just like Charlemagne's crown, this sceptre was made for one man only and would fit nobody else.

The Venlo and Wittmundhafen squadrons were formed shortly afterwards. My name did not appear on the list of postings to these squadrons, nor did those of Herbert and Fritz. We were marked down for other duties, our new commanding officer, Toni Thaler, told us, and so we continued our test flying from Bad Zwischenahn, and were satisfied with our lot.

Then, one afternoon, we were treated to our first uninvited visit from "the other side"—two Mosquitoes from the R.A.F. were circling high above our field and apparently taking pictures at their ease. We tried our best to get permission from Thaler to go up and spoil their fun—there were at least four combat-ready Komets in our hangar which only needed tanking up—but our pleas were unheeded. Thaler refused point blank. He did not have official permission to permit us to undertake an interception sortie, and he was certainly not going to take such responsibility on his own shoulders. Our blood boiled. We knew that Späte would have given the necessary permission and would probably have gone up there himself as well. But there was nothing that we could do about it.

We did not have long to wait for a sequel to the intrusion of the Mosquitoes. All hell broke loose that same afternoon! The sirens started howling shortly after dinner and, as per instructions, we made our way to the vicinity of the air-raid shelters. Enemy bomber formations now seemed to be coming from every direction, the sun glinting on scores of escorting fighters. The anti-aircraft guns around the field fired away without pause, and dozens of harmless-looking smoke balls blossomed among the neat formations of Fortresses.

B-17 Flying Fortress

Then, two direct hits! Two Fortresses began to break up immediately above our heads, and nine ... ten ... eleven parachutes mushroomed in the blue sky and gently floated away to the east. Like an enormous maple seed, the severed wing from one of the bombers fluttered down in front of our eyes, ripping through the shrouds of one of the luckless parachutists like a knife through butter.

Then there was a shout—"Look out, low-level attack!" and as our heads spun round we found ourselves virtually looking down the gun barrels of a pair of Mustangs sweeping in over the forest. Four of us dived for dear life behind a pile of gravel as both fighters opened up, their bullets swathing across the field—and then they were gone! Cautiously, we raised our heads. The dust kicked up by the bullets was just settling, and the wall of the station radio hut just behind us was perforated by a neat row of holes barely a metre from the ground. Behind this wall were four of our Signal Corps girls, but fortunately they had been lying flat on the floor, and although somewhat shaken, they were none the worse for wear.

"Rotten bastards!" commented Fritz, who was beating the dust from his trousers. "I only collected these pants from the cleaners yesterday, and now look at 'em! Rotten bastards!"

One of the blonde young Signal Corps girls, seeing Fritz's chagrin, called: "Give them to me, Fritz, and I'll sponge and iron them for you!"

Fritz acknowledged her kind offer with a dismal gesture and replied: "Can't be done, sweetie! My only other pair are at the cleaners now, and I can't very well wander around in my underpants!"

So ended our first visit from "the other side". Fortunately for us, the "heavy stuff" had apparently been headed elsewhere, but we knew that we were not going to be as lucky as this every time.

Hardly an hour after the departure of the enemy aircraft, I was ordered to collect a few urgently needed parts and fly them to Olenjik's squadron at Wittmundhafen in a Bf 110. I thoroughly enjoyed the short flight over the East Frisian forests and fields, and soon found myself landing at an *operational* Komet base. As I made my approach, I saw an Me 163B standing poised for take-off at the end of the runway. I landed and taxied the Bf 110 away to the workshop hangar. "Who's taking-off, then?" I asked one of my mechanics who had come to unload my cargo.

"It's Captain Olejnik, Sir!—he replied. "Our first take-off from here!"

At that moment the combustion chamber of Olenjik's Komet shot out a cloud of steam and, a split-second later with a muffled crack the fuel had ignited, the steam giving place to a brilliant bayonet of patterned flame. The intense roar grew louder as Olejnik switched from first to second thrust stage, and the whole field seemed to reverberate as, with the third thrust stage, the Komet began to move. Although I had witnessed just such a scene many times before—in fact, almost daily for a long time—my eyes followed the Me 163B's progress just as though I was seeing it all for the first time. "Hope he'll make it all right!" I thought to myself as Olenjik's aircraft dropped its wheels and shot up steeply into the sky.

"He's O.K. now," I thought, and I was just about to turn back to my Bf 110 when, at about three thousand metres and still in a steep climb, Olejnik's Komet faltered. The rocket began to stutter, and thick irregular clouds of steam shot from the tailpipe. Olejnik held his climb for a few moments more, then levelled off and presumably tried to re-start the rocket motor. For a second or so there was neither smoke nor steam behind the Komet's tail, and then the combustion chamber shot out a white stream which rapidly changed to an ominous black. "Bale out!" I screamed, and then I noticed a whitish spray from Olejnik's emergency fuel-dumping release. Streaming T-stoff, the Komet swung back towards the airfield. The cockpit canopy flew off and spun down to earth. "About time!" I thought, expecting to see Olejnik follow the canopy. But, no! The Komet came lower and lower, making a wide, slow circuit of the field before turning in for a landing approach. But all was not well. The aircraft seemed to stagger, and now began to fall, faster and faster. Olejnik tried valiantly to level off again, and then she was down! Not softly in a con-trolled landing, but like a stone, rebounding into the air, and then hitting the ground again. The port wing dug in and the Komet spun wildly like a top. A body flew out of the aircraft and, almost simultaneously, there was a vivid red splash of flame followed by a cloud of white steam.

I could not find a lorry to take me across the airfield, but the fire tender and the ambulance, already alerted during Olejnik's erratic flight, were on the spot almost at once, and streams of water doused the smoking wreck while the ambulance attendants hurried across to where Olejnik's body lay, carefully lifted him on to a stretcher and hurried across to the ambulance. "Hell!" I thought, "What bloody awful luck!" Olejnik was an experienced fighter pilot who, decorated with the Knight's Cross of the Iron Cross, had several dozen victories to his credit. A first-class chap from every angle and part of the Komet "team" virtually from the start, and now he had to cop it in this fashion, on the threshold of showing what this revolutionary warplane with which he had lived so long could really do!

I sat in the airfield control tower, gloomy and depressed, chain-smoking cigarettes, and anxiously awaiting a ring from the telephone, yet at the same time dreading it. At last it did ring, and one of the others grabbed the phone. After a moment, he put down the receiver and said: "He's in luck! A broken vertebra. Nothing dangerous!"

Yes, that's the way we had become. If you *only* broke a vertebra you were lucky! We were certainly becoming pretty hard-boiled.

Back at Bad Zwischenahn I rummaged in a carefully-locked cupboard and pulled out a bottle of good brandy. I filled Fritz's, Herbert's and my own glasses, and we drank a toast: "To Olejnik's damaged backbone!" Hans Bott and Franz Medicus joined our company—Hans for the brandy and Franz for the conversation. Hans was one of the most daring of Komet pilots, and quite a fellow with his slide-rule when he wanted to know something absolutely exactly. I believe that he was the first man to perform a forward loop in the Komet, at least, at Bad Zwischenahn, but he was unhappy in his love life, or his fiancée was too far away, and brandy *consoled* him. Franz was one of the most enthusiastic sailplane pilots in Germany, and there was nothing in his world but gliding and his family. Eisenmann, Mühlstroh and Glogner played Skat in a corner—Jupp cheating as usual and protesting his innocence volubly—while Nelte and Oeltjen played chess. The others—and there were not many of them since the operational squadrons at Venlo and Wittmundhafen had denuded our mess—wrote letters. Hans Bott had already packed his kit and was trying to figure out a way of organizing a trip to Berlin on the sly before joining the unit to which he had been posted.

"You can come with me tomorrow, Hans! There is still a spare seat in my Messerschmitt 108. Why don't you ask the old man?" offered Herbert.

Me 108 "Taifun"

"What the hell are you going to Berlin again for?" grumbled Fritz, jealous of Herbert's trip.

"I must see the General of Fighters—orders!"

"Well, tell him he should send our Späte back to us!"

And so it went on—the desultory conversation of a mess with a shadow hanging over it. We were tired and dispirited. Soon we finished the last of the brandy, and somehow Fritz, Herbert and I all managed to pile on to my 125-cc. D.K.W. motor-cycle and, looking rather like an overloaded shopping bag, we swayed into Bad Zwischenahn and made for our billets. Before going our own ways we stood and chatted for a while, however.

"If you have a chance, ask the General about Späte when you see him tomorrow, will you, Herbert! Maybe he can get him transferred back to us again. Certainly we have never needed him so much as we need him now, what with Pitz and Olejnik laid up in hospital, probably for months!"

"I'll see what I can do," said Herbert, "if the 'old un' has a little time for me and is not surrounded by a bevy of chair-borne warriors!"

I pushed my motor-cycle into the little chicken house next to the Dyckerhoff's home where I was billeted, and climbed silently up the stairs to my room.

The pitiless alarm clock shattered my slumbers at six o'clock the next morning—how short the nights seemed to have become—and I staggered out of bed and peered out the window at Bad Zwischenahn's characteristic morning fog. To us, of course, this fog was a most disagreeable phenomenon for it meant more time to languish in the low-pressure chamber and for theoretical instruction. It took the sun some hours usually to burn off this blanket.

When I reached the airfield Herbert was standing in the preflight check room of the control tower in impotent fury! He could not get permission to take-off owing to the fog.

"You could damned well let me go," he stormed at the controller who happened to be a civilian, "as you know that it is clear at two hundred metres! Damn it all," he added, "in Russia nobody gave a damn for a bit of ground fog!"

"Sorry, but I can't let you go all the same, Langer, and you know that just as well as I do!" The controller added that if it would keep him happy Herbert could go over to the met boys' hut and take a look at their charts.

But the weather charts did not look in the least healthy. On the contrary, fog was spreading all the way to Hanover and over half of Lüneburg Heath. Only the area around Brunswick and Magdeburg seemed to be clear, but Berlin itself and the whole area surrounding it was buried deep in "soup". The chap in charge of the weather station did his best for us, and, with our heads together, we studied the pattern as it existed and the changes that were to be expected on Herbert's flight route, but the charts showed no likelihood of any clearance that day, although the senior meteorological man— who had planned to accompany Herbert to Berlin for a birthday celebration and had his case standing ready for the trip under his desk—promised to phone Berlin every thirty minutes to see if there was any change.

Outside the met office we could not even see the windsock drooping at the top of its ten-metre pole.

"It makes you sick, this weather," Herbert grumbled, "and if it hasn't cleared in an hour I swear that I'll fly blind all the way to Berlin!"

"Don't be a bloody fool!" I said. "To listen to you anybody would think that the General is awaiting your arrival with bated breath! Send them a teleprinter message telling them that you'll arrive tomorrow."

But Herbert would have none of it. "I'll get there today if I have to run there on my two legs!" he insisted as he left me at the door of the low-pressure chamber.

12

Herbert's Number Comes Up

As I LEFT the low-pressure chamber a good hour later, visibility had increased to about a kilometre, but only just. However, there were signs that the warm sunshine was beginning to break through the thin veil of fog, so it looked as though Herbert might be lucky after all. I strolled over to the met. hut where I was told that Herbert had taken off for Berlin some ten minutes earlier.

"And how's the weather?" I asked.

"Patchy! We tried to stop him but he refused to hang around any longer. Hanover and Heide are still closed in, and farther south it's foggy as well. He'll have to fly over that lot, but Berlin has improved a bit."

I glanced over the weather charts and decided that, in similar circumstances, I should probably have taken off as well.

I left the met. hut and walked across to the rocket test hangar which, as usual, was full of white steam. Two or three new Me 163Bs were now arriving each day and, already test-flown by Karl Voy, had to be tested once more at Bad Zwischenahn before being passed over to one of the operational squadrons of which there were now three. At that time Venlo had only four aircraft, Wittmundhafen had six, and the

Zwischenahn squadron, which officially did not exist but was here all the same, had no aircraft of its own at all and flew whatever happened to be available.

When I entered the big hangar, one of the new Komets was just about to undergo a static test run, so I went over, climbed in and settled down at the controls. Otto Oertzen, chief of the "rocket laundry", stood on the ladder alongside the cockpit, and we were ready for the fun to commence. Squatting there with the infernal noise of a thousand devils behind you, their howling reaching a tremendous crescendo as the thrust lever was pushed fully forward, may not have been everybody's idea of a pleasant pastime, but for me it was an indescribable thrill; a feeling of untold power gripped me and I might have been Thor himself controlling the thunder and lightning. The strong walls of the test hangar shook and the solid floor plates which held the stay wires quivered, T-stoff and C-stoff surged through tiny pipes towards their devilish marriage in the combustion chamber, and then, barely four minutes later, a muffled bang announced the end of my "ride" and there was deathly quiet. Otto Oertzen was beaming all over his face as he did whenever a test run was completed successfully.

"Care to flight-test it?" he asked. He didn't have to ask a second time and an hour later, after reporting my intended flight to Thaler, I was climbing into the cockpit of the "new bird" which had been freshly tanked up and was ready to go. This particular specimen of the Komet was one of the first to have an armament of two 30-mm. MK 108 cannon which had replaced the 20-mm. "peashooters" of the early machines. These were located in the wing roots, and the ammunition, sixty rounds per cannon, was carried in two boxes under a detachable fairing behind the radio mast. Two air bottles for cocking the guns were mounted, one behind and one below each weapon, and the guns were controlled by a conventional firing button in the top of the control column. The guns were aimed by means of a standard Revi 16B gunsight which was attached to a removable mounting at the base of the windscreen.

There was a target floating in the middle of the Zwischenahn Lake, and I was told to try out the new cannon while I was at it, as this Me 163B was already earmarked for the squadron based at Venlo.

The rocket motor fired as efficiently as it had in the test hangar an hour earlier. I pushed the thrust lever fully forward to the third stage, there was a slight jerk as the aircraft jumped over the restraining blocks, and away I went. By that time, the fog bank had almost completely evaporated, merely a few milky shreds floating close to the ground. Once past the two thousand-metre mark, I settled down to enjoy the climb. When the motor finally cut, I levelled off, performed a few high-spirited rolls, pushed the nose down to gather speed, and then pulled up again until the Komet was all but stalling. A series of wide spirals around the town followed, and then I aimed the aircraft at the Zwischenahn Lake. I could see the floating target quite clearly. I flicked on the Revi sight and fired! I had miscalculated my first burst, the shells striking to port of the target. I depressed the firing button again, but my port cannon jammed immediately. I had been concentrating so much on the target that I only just managed to pull out of my dive over the surface of the lake! The Komet gained a little altitude and I made it to the field, but I had to come in rather low, and I had only just sufficient speed in hand to clear the airfield perimeter! My landing approach was extremely ropey but, with luck on my side, I managed to put the aircraft down diagonally against the wind. The Komet skidded along the ground and finally came to a halt with no damage done! Phew! That was close!

A landing like that was simply asking for trouble, and I prepared myself for another explosion from Toni Thaler. The towing vehicle was already on its way to the spot where I had come to a standstill, and among the troop of mechanics I could see Fritz Kelb and Sergeant Nelte. Strangely, they didn't fool around as usual, and none of them shouted any sarcastic remarks about my appalling landing. Fritz was the first to reach my plane, and he stood before me with grave eyes.

"You'd better hold tight, Mano," he said quietly, and, of course, still thinking about my bloody awful landing, I shouted back gaily: "Don't worry, Fritz. I shall not become too big-headed!"

But Fritz only looked at me in a strange, detached way, his eyes looking through me as though his thoughts were far away. Finally, he almost whispered: "Herbert's dead, Mano!"

Then he turned away, directing the lifting vehicle as it backed up to my aircraft. I stood there for a moment, paralyzed with shock. He glanced in my direction and, in answer to my unspoken question, said: "Emergency landing in fog northwest of Hanover. Probably a belly landing. Broken neck and legs. His two passengers killed as well. I don't know any more!"

As we walked back behind the lifting vehicle which had now raised the Komet, telescopic arms secured firmly under the wings and the landing skid resting between two short caterpillar tracks, he told me that a

Me 163 Lifting vehicle

couple of farmworkers had discovered the Bf 108 between some fruit trees, and that all three were still in their seats without visible injuries—but they were dead! So our Herbert would never get to see the General of Fighters after all. And then I thought of Helga! I should have to break the news to her.

Deep in thought, our shoulders hunched with dejection, we walked on in silence—right across the take-off runway! There was a shout which brought us back from our thoughts, and we suddenly realized that, at the far end of the runway, an Me 163B was about to take-off, and we were in its path!

"Strasnicky—his fifth sharp start!" shouted Fritz as we ran as fast as our legs could carry us, the Komet already screaming towards us like a bat out of hell! Then he was off the ground; his wheels were dancing away barely fifty metres from us. The nose of the Komet came up just over the airfield boundary.

"There's something wrong!" said Fritz quietly, taking the very words from my mouth. The rocket motor was making an unusual noise. Hardly noticeable, yet not the normal full-throated roar. By that time our ears were so finely attuned to the Walter rocket that we could detect the very slightest "off" note like a conductor with his strings. Then everything seemed to happen at once. Still climbing, the Komet emitted an immense cloud of smoke—first white, then black, followed almost immediately by a jagged flame. The aircraft, by that time at an altitude of about three thousand metres, flew horizontally for a brief moment, and we saw the cockpit canopy whirl away, and then the nose jerked up and the aircraft fell away and went into a steep dive. At that moment, Strasnicky's body flew out of the cockpit. His parachute mushroomed open, and he was saved!

"Look out, Fritz!" I shouted. While we had been watching Strasnicky swinging from his parachute shrouds, the burning Me 163 had banked around and was now diving straight at us! We ran for a few yards, looking over our shoulders in horror, and then flattened ourselves on the ground. I was sure that at any moment that Komet was going to land smack on the back of our necks. But as though piloted by some invisible hand, the burning wreck pulled out of its dive, banked steeply to starboard, and hit the ground a few seconds later well outside the perimeter of the airfield. A thick, whitish-grey pyre of smoke ascended behind the young fir trees, its edges flushed with the glow from hungry red flames that were busily consuming all that was left of another of our Komets!

"That was just about all we needed to make our

day!" muttered Fritz as he retrieved his cap. We looked up and saw that the wind was carrying Sergeant Strasnicky right towards the Zwischenahn Lake. We could see his feet kicking as he disappeared behind the tall trees bordering the lake, and when, after a sprint, we reached the shore, they had already fished him out of the water. None the worse for his experience, Nicky told us that his fire warning light was already flashing at five hundred metres altitude, and the cockpit was filling with acrid smoke. When it started getting as hot as hell, he had decided that it was time to get out!

Why couldn't poor old Herbert Langer have had a little luck like Nicky had enjoyed a few minutes earlier? His life had been hanging literally by a silken thread. The Komet could have exploded in the air before he had extricated himself from the cockpit—he could have been overcome by the smoke—his parachute could have caught fire or failed to open! It seemed to be rapidly becoming the rule that the worse the situation the more chance one had of surviving! Those ridiculous accidents that had cost men their lives! Joschi grazing a Flak tower! Wörndl—probably one careless second. And then Herbert! All snuffed out like candles. It seemed that the Grim Reaper only swung her scythe when its victim felt safe!

At about 18.00 hours I reached Oldenburg, catching Helga at her office just as she was preparing to leave for home.

"Oh, it's you, Mano! I was just going to call the airfield to ask if Herbert had returned. I've managed to get hold of a couple of very special tickets for the theatre this evening—'Love and Intrigue' with Schmitt-hammer playing the rôle of Worm—I know Herbert will adore it!"

She stood in front of a small mirror combing her auburn hair as she prattled on. My mouth had gone dry and a lump seemed to block my throat.

"You know what, Mano? If by any chance Herbert hasn't got back from Berlin, you'll escort me to the theatre, won't you? We'll call Hilda and tell her, and then she can phone Herbert so that he can meet us after the play!"

Somehow I found my tongue, and croaked: "Herbert cannot meet us after the theatre tonight, Helga!"

She fumbled with her lipstick. "But why ever not? Has he been kept in Berlin?"

I cleared my throat desperately. I felt awkward and foolish, and as she turned towards me I felt as faint-hearted and helpless as a schoolboy caught in the act of making some mischief. I was totally inadequate for this sort of thing.

"Herbert had some bad luck, Helga. He had to make an emergency landing near Hanover because of the fog this morning, and . . ." my voice deteriorated into a croak. But Helga had no forebodings and continued chattering away gaily about the many emergency landings Herbert had told her he had made, and how exciting some of them must have been. Then she pouted her lips and said: "Well, at least he could have called me!"

I finally gathered the last vestiges of my courage and blurted out: "He couldn't call you, Helga. He's dead!"

For a moment she stared at me with large, unbelieving eyes, then the colour drained from her face. She gripped the desk beside her, her knuckles showing white, and then she slowly sat down. The look of sheer misery on her beautiful face was pitiful to see. She sat in utter silence for a few moments, and then she whispered: "Did he have to suffer?"

I reassured her. Then I helped her to her feet and took her to her home. She didn't say a word as we walked. Then, at her door, she tried to say something but her voice would just not come! Her eyes full of tears, she wrenched open the door and ran inside the house. My own eyes were filled with tears as I collected my motor-cycle and rode back to the field.

13

A Visit to Venlo

BAD LUCK seems never to come in small packages, and a few days later Fritz Kelb was transferred to Böhner's squadron at Venlo. I immediately made an official application to Thaler for a transfer to Venlo, but he turned down my request on the grounds that Böhner's squadron was already at full strength and, in any case, I was to be given other duties shortly. Only a half-hour after leaving Thaler's office I learned from Franz that he too had been transferred—to Wittmundhafen. Now all my closest friends had been killed or posted! If I couldn't get myself posted to Venlo I was determined to at least visit the base, and once there perhaps I could talk to Böhner in person to see if he could wangle me a posting.

Finally I succeeded in finding an excuse to fly one of our hack Bf 110s to Venlo. As soon as I arrived I sensed that the whole atmosphere of the base was oppressive! Although the squadron had already flown more than a dozen interception missions with its Komets, nobody had managed to touch an enemy plane as yet, let alone shoot one down! The reports from Wittmundhafen were much the same—emergency take-offs, no contact with the enemy, and return to base!

It had soon become evident that these failures were caused primarily by adhering to the book; using fighter-control arrangements similar to those that we had practised for so many months at Bad Zwischenahn. What had seemed to function perfectly during training broke down completely under operational conditions. The fast-climbing Me 163s were simply *too* fast for the ground-control methods that, basically, had been developed for use with orthodox piston-engined fighters. It was true that our Freya radar was registering the approach of every high-flying enemy aircraft without fail, but that was as far as it went. As soon as the Komet had to change its course at high altitudes—and this proved to be necessary every time it was sent up!—the whole system broke down completely. The fault, and an exasperating one it was, lay with our compass. It spun like a top in a high-speed turn, and after receiving his new heading, a pilot had to fly straight and level for a while to steady the wildly spinning compass. Only then could he start looking for his new bearings, and one could hardly expect a Mosquito to hang around and wait for you!

Mosquito Bomber

During the two days prior to my arrival at Venlo, Fritz and his companions had taken off five or six times, and each time they had not even fired their guns in anger! Their rage and feeling of impotence may well be imagined. For months they learned the A-B-C of the

Komet forwards and backwards, only to be stumped by this ridiculous defect of the compass. Fritz and I sat together the whole evening trying to think of a solution to the problem, but if our technicians had been unable to come up with an answer, what hope had we got?

The next day, just as I was about to order the ground staff to prepare my Bf 110 for my return flight to Bad Zwischenahn, there was a preliminary alarm, followed by reports of a large bomber formation heading in our direction. Otto Böhner had three Komets at readiness on the main runway, and as further reports indicated that the intruding formation was still pointing directly at Venlo, the opportunity was too good to be missed. I told the ground staff to push my Bf 110 under some camouflage netting, and drove out to the starting line. Fritz and two other pilots were already seated in their cockpits waiting for the order to take-off. It was a sweltering hot day, and Fritz had left his cockpit canopy open, so I squatted on the wing beside the cockpit. He had not fastened his oxygen mask, and his face revealed no excitement. Only his lips were dry, and from time to time he moistened them with his tongue, while his eyes continually searched the sky above.

"You just wait, Mano. We'll blood the Komet today if those bastards don't turn away! This time I'll fly by sight only, and the devil take the hindmost if I don't find 'em!"

"Don't be too rash, Fritz," I cautioned. "A stack of bombers like that is not a girl's boarding school, you know. If you don't catch 'em today, then there is always tomorrow!"

"If necessary, I'll take on the bloody girls boarding school as well!"

At that moment we saw the bombers—high up over the Dutch countryside. Thin white lines in orderly rank and file, their contrails streaming back for miles. In fact, it was the contrails that we were looking at, for the bombers were so high that they were no more than minute dots at the extreme tips of the trails.

Fritz evidently received an R/T message, for he

pulled on his oxygen mask and raised his hand to
signal the starter vehicle. I slammed his cockpit canopy
shut, and before pulling down his goggles, he winked
at me through the perspex and gave me the "thumbs
up". He tested his controls for free play and then
punched the starter button. A few seconds later the
stabbing "third stage" flame shot out from the tailpipe,
his wheels jumped over the tiny blocks, and the madly
roaring Komet was flashing down the runway, gaining
speed with every yard. Then it shot away like a flaming
arrow. I followed Fritz's aircraft with my eyes until it
disappeared from view. I then transferred my gaze to
the spreading bunch of contrails, now almost directly
over the airfield.

One anxious minute followed another, but the silvery trails moved steadily on across the sky. The other
two Komets had taken off directly after that flown by
Fritz, but there was no sign of them either. Then it
happened! A bunch of white lines, so clean and orderly
a moment before, seemed to waver, two breaking away
to port and one to starboard. A few seconds later I
distinctly heard the muffled sound of rapid cannon
fire. Then it came again. Almost at once there was a
bizarre, ragged puff of smoke in the sky which before-
hand had been spotless except for the contrails. It
was way below and behind the main formation—an
explosion! The cloud seemed to expand jerkily, and
two . . . three, no, four parachutes appeared as though
by magic. Almost simultaneously the white cloud began to
spill a shower of dark fragments that fell rapidly, followed by a burning wing which left a dark spiral of
smoke. And there was the fuselage with the other wing
still attached, turning over and over. The wreckage,
clearly recognizable as the remains of some large aircraft,
fell faster and faster, until it slammed into the ground
far beyond the airfield. The Komet had drawn blood!

Elated, we awaited anxiously the return of the trio
of Komets. The first Messerschmitt appeared a few
minutes later, soared a good thousand metres above
the airfield, plunged towards the ground in a dive,

pulled up again, and began its final approach, trailing a long plume of white smoke. We leaped on to the starting vehicle and raced to the point where we expected the Komet to touch down. The fire tender raced across from the other side of the field, but the Messerschmitt made a perfectly normal landing, and skidded to a halt on the soft grass verge.

The pilot of the Komet proved to be Schametz, a young sergeant from Vienna. Relieved and furious at the same time, he clambered from the cockpit while the fire tender doused his steaming plane with water. His face was reddened by T-stoff steam, and tears were streaming from his inflamed eyes, and he gave vent to his feelings in no uncertain fashion, proving to possess a superlative vocabulary of choice Austrian curses! It seems that his rocket motor had cut when he was hardly a thousand metres from the bomber formation. He had struggled to restart the motor but, in no time at all, was all but overcome by the "tear gas" streaming into his cockpit and forcing him to return without firing his cannon. He hadn't seen hide nor hair of Fritz, but almost as he finished his report another Komet made a clean landing on the field, followed immediately by a third.

"Learned a lot, Mano!" Fritz had a sour face as he climbed from his cockpit. We walked around his aircraft. "Look at this," he said, indicating countless rents and holes in both wing leading edges, and dents in the armoured nose cone. "It was like a ruddy hailstorm, I tell you!"

He examined some damage where a bullet had just touched an elevon. A fraction of an inch lower and Fritz might well have lost control of the aircraft at a crucial moment.

"Then who shot that Fortress down?" I asked.

"The flak! A direct hit. It was straggling behind on its own, and I was just about to make a pass at it when the whole blasted formation started up at me, punching my kite full of holes!"

We walked slowly across the field, and Fritz continued: "We can't attack a stack of bombers like that from the rear—it's ruddy suicide! You get such a plastering from hundreds of point fives that you forget to press the tit! The trouble was that I climbed too high and my rocket had cut, so I could only get at 'em from the behind."

We were silent for a while, but I am sure that our minds were both concentrated on the one problem—how to penetrate the vicious crossfire thrown up by those Fortress formations.

"We ought to try slamming rockets into them," Fritz said suddenly, "from a greater distance away and, best of all, from head-on or at an oblique angle from below!"

"You can forget rockets while Hachtel is still enamoured with those 30-mm. cannon, though heavens knows when we will succeed in getting them to function properly," I replied.

Lieutenant Hachtel had been transferred to us only a short time earlier to serve as our weapons test officer. He had accumulated quite an amount of experience

Ju 87G-1 with 37 mm. BK (Flak 18) Cannon

knocking out tanks with his Junkers 87 and was suppos-
edly giving us the benefit of this in evaluating the
Komet. As far as he was concerned the 30-mm. MK
108 cannon was the very last word in effectiveness—or
should be. However, he had still to make his point in so
far as we were concerned, and nothing useful had
materialized from Hachtel's presence.

"The MK 108 is too bloody unreliable," said Fritz
vociferously. "It's too damned temperamental by half.
One of them feels like pumping out a few shells
occasionally, but most of the time both of them are
jammed solid, and you're lucky if you have managed to
get off one decent burst."

At this moment we arrived at the operations hut
where Otto Böhner was about to climb into his car,
evidently on his way to look at the crashed Fortress.
Fritz bade me farewell and joined him, and it was time
for me to collect my Bf 110 and leave once more for
Bad Zwischenahn. My short visit to Venlo had only
made me still more discontented. Why the hell couldn't
I be there, in Böhner's squadron, together with Fritz
again? I made up my mind as I winged my way back to
Bad Zwischenahn that I should confront Thaler again,
and if he still wouldn't transfer me to Venlo, then I
should write to Späte in person and persuade him to
use his influence on my behalf. What could Thaler's
motive be for keeping me kicking my heels at Bad
Zwischenahn? It could only be the antagonism that had
sprung up between us that day months before. The
sooner I settled this little difference of opinion once
and for all, the better it would be.

As soon as I landed I headed in the direction of
the commanding officer's office, spoiling for a showdown,
but halfway there I bumped into Nelte, the tallest of
our sergeant-pilots, who quickly took all the wind out
of my sails. Nelte looked most woebegone, so I said:
"What's up with you, Nelte? From your face I should
say that you have just been sucking sour lemons!"

"I feel every bit as miserable as I probably look,

Sir," he replied. "We can both stick combat flying into our Sunday hats!"

"I don't understand you, Nelte. What's that supposed to mean?"

"You just wander along and see Thaler. He's already waiting for you! We have both been posted to Jesau as production test pilots!"

"Nonsense, Nelte! They have got Voy, Perschell and Lamm at Jesau now. They can't possibly want any more pilots to test fly the new crates."

"Of course, you wouldn't have heard, Lieutenant. Lamm crashed only yesterday, and Voy and Perschall can't manage the job on their own. We are supposed to leave for Jesau at the crack of dawn tomorrow to join the not-so-happy bunch of production test pilots."

I could hardly believe my ears. If Nelte was telling me the truth then Thaler was really gunning for me. We had a number of fully trained Komet pilots by this time, but all of them were newcomers by comparison with Nelte and me. Thaler could have posted any of them to Jesau, but, no, he had picked us, knowing full well that there was nothing we wanted more than a posting to an operational squadron.

I was boiling over with resentment and rage when I stalked into his office. I intimated that I was reporting back from Venlo, and, hardly able to contain myself, awaited his invitation to make a detailed report as was customary. But Thaler merely glanced up at me, and then passed over my posting orders, saying: "Ziegler, you have been transferred to Jesau, and you are to report to the chief production test pilot there, Herr Voy, at 08.00 hours the day after tomorrow. You will be subordinate to Voy until you receive a recall!"

"As far as I know, Captain," I said in impotent fury, "an officer can never be subordinate to a civilian!"

But Thaler did not even trouble to look up at me, and merely said: "Of course, you will still be under orders from the Test-Commando in so far as the military side of your new assignment is concerned. You are subordinate to Voy only as regards the test flying, as he is responsible for the whole programme at Jesau."

"But, Captain, Nelte and I want to go to an operational unit—in fact Späte had earmarked us for combat duties long ago."

"That is no concern of mine, Ziegler. They need two experienced pilots in Jesau, and I can only recommend you two, all the others have already been posted to Venlo or Wittmundhafen."

Thaler knew damned well that there were plenty of pilots that could have been assigned to this job, and he seemed to expect some new objection from me for, before I could say anything further, he added: "You know, of course, that Jesau is not exactly the ideal airfield. It is, in fact, only nine hundred metres in length. We need new Komets urgently now, and Voy and Perschall cannot manage on their own. But in any case your posting is an order, Ziegler, and I assume that you know what that means."

He paused, and then went on: "After all, it is only a *temporary* posting, and I trust that I shall be able to transfer you to an operational unit soon. In any case, we are all moving to Brandis within the next few days."

I was sure that he was being sarcastic when he gave me an encouraging smile and wished me "Hals-und Beinbruch!"* as he dismissed me from his presence.

Thoroughly dejected, I walked aimlessly about the airfield after leaving Thaler and, without any conscious desire to head in that direction, eventually found myself at the starting point for our "sharp" flights on the east side of the field. As I stood there I recalled my first "sharp" take-off from this spot, and both the naked fear of my incalculable rocket motor and the indescribable delight of soaring high in the heavens came back to me. Now all those months of training

*"Hals-und Beinbruch" means literally "Broken neck and legs", standard among Luftwaffe pilots of wishing "Good luck and happy landings!"

began to seem so much wasted effort. I felt as useless as a spent firework.

I strolled on, past the radio hut which still showed the scars left by the bullets of the intruding Mustangs, and the solid air raid shelter for which we had headed at the double whenever we believed that "they" were making for our field at last. A few hundred metres beyond the shelter stood the engine test hangar, still boiling and roaring as noisily as ever—it was difficult to believe that within a few days this hangar, which had sent its unearthly wailing into the ether for so long, would stand silent and empty. And for me? Jesau in East Prussia, not far from Königsberg. Now that was a safe area for anybody that wanted it that way. Far from the front line, no air raid warnings, in fact, a real rest cure! Flying day after day in brand new aircraft without a shell in their ammunition boxes, and evening after evening of Skat with Karl Voy, Franz Perschall and Nelte in some God-forsaken hut or other! I knew the blasted place only too well as for months on end I had ferried Bf 109s from there to Pori in Finland. Jesau! The blasted end of the world. "Come to Jesau for the sheer boredom of it!" "Jesau: Guaranteed to bore you to death!" Oh well, it was obvious that I was going to have to make the best of a bad job. The Komets had got to be tested and I would test 'em to the best of my ability.

At that moment a glowing white rocket exhaust stabbed out from the wall behind the engine test hangar, hissing over the burned grass and screaming away in the twilight. I stood a hundred metres away, the jagged flame straight ahead of me. The hot breath of the rocket motor embraced me, the powerful waves of heat pounding on my chest and shaking me like a leaf. There was a muffled crack and the fire died out, the heat waves ebbed and everything was quiet once more. My anger had evaporated with the last of the T-stoff in that rocket motor, and I was resigned to my posting.

On the way to the mess I remembered that there

was something important that I had to do before departing from Bad Zwischenahn—there was still much of the eighty litres of plum brandy which we had so carefully transported from Bolzen in an immense glass balloon protected by a wickerwork basket. We had stored the balloon in Hanna's cellar to which I promptly repaired. Hanna agreed to give me a hand with my task, and we filled bottle after bottle from the tremendous container, while the fumes gradually took their effect. In fact, we were soon laughing and joking as though we had been out on a binge. Then our task completed, I presented a bottle of the brandy to Hanna, and set off to see Hilda and Helmut Dyckerhoff to break my news. They could not have been more upset had I been their own son. Helmut hurried down to his cellar to procure the finest bottle that he could find, and for several hours we talked over old times.

Early next morning a gang of us went down to the town to fetch the bottles from Hanna's cellar and transported them to our mess with due ceremony and reverence. We had just got the bottles stored away when, at ten o'clock, the air-raid sirens began to howl. We ran pell-mell from the field and, grabbing my D.K.W., I drove at top speed to the other side of the lake. And then they came—countless black dots trailing their familiar contrails. A mass of bombs came screaming down, and the airfield disappeared in a rain of destruction, the earth heaving and great fountains of dirt reaching into the sky. The scream of flashing steel blotted out the life of our airfield and, with the roar of engines diminishing in the distance, we could see that only desolation remained. Uprooted trees lay drunkenly against their more fortunate fellows which had merely been stripped of their leaves and branches; the whole field looked as though it had been churned over by some fantastic plough, and the hangars had disappeared in piles of twisted steel and rubble. And the mess ... I could not help laughing for I suddenly remembered that stack of bottles of plum brandy that we had so carefully carried up from Bad Zwischenahn an hour or so before and, below those bottles, the packets and packets of saccharine awaiting transportation to our good friend Valentini!

14

Production Flight Testing

THE TRAIN from Königsberg to Jesau rumbled along its track as of old, and the surrounding landscape was already so familiar to me that I scarcely bothered to give it a glance. It was only when, out of the corner of my eye, I saw a mighty maintenance hangar and a good dozen brand new Me 163Bs still resplendent in their fresh varnish, that my spirits rose a little. At the field Karl Voy appeared from beneath the wing of a Komet, smiles all over his face. We shook hands, and he said: "I am very glad that you are here, Mano. We simply cannot manage this shop on our own any longer. Where's Nelte?"

"Coming on the next train from Königsberg," I answered. "He has a girl-friend there."

Voy smiled, and then said seriously: "You had better prepare yourself for a shock, Mano. The field here is nothing but an uneven patch. It's much too short and as rough as a potato field."

"You don't need to tell me anything about this damned field, Karl! I've made a few hundred take-offs and landings with Bf 109s from here, and I know only too well what a stinker it is. With good brakes and more than a bit of luck, you can pull up about fifty metres from the fence!"

"Then you had better get used to the pleasant fact that, in wet weather, we are mightily relieved if we stop within twenty, no, ten metres of the damned fence. It's not so bad when it's dry. Then you have a reserve of about two hundred metres, but when it rains you had better touch down slap in the centre of that landing cross, or even in front of it. Otherwise you'll find yourself wearing the palings of that fence as a collar."

I looked sceptically at the fence that set bounds to the narrow northside end of the short runway. This was the only fence of such a height that I had ever seen on any airfield, and in its time it had attracted a vast amount of invective from those unlucky enough to fly from the field. Behind the fence was the furrowed, bumpy ground of an old stone quarry, leaving little doubt in one's mind as to the result of crashing through those palings! I had sworn at the fence heartily enough when I had landed a Bf 109 at Jesau, but at least the Bf 109 had wheels and brakes—the Komet had neither!

"Come with me to the take-off point," suggested Voy. "Perschall is just about to make a towed start, and you may as well have a look at the whole layout in peace while you have the chance."

As the Bf 110 was still being tanked up, we took our time over walking the few hundred metres separating us from the take-off point, and I told Voy about the tragic end of Bad Zwischenahn. Franz Perschall was standing beside his Komet, watching our approach. I liked Perschall a lot. He was one of those matter-of-fact fellows who rarely complain and take on the most dangerous of jobs without much ado. He flew with as much calm and self-assurance as a baker shovelling loaves into an oven. At Bad Zwischenahn, the Komet had looked an innocent lamb in Perschall's hands. And then the engines of the Bf 110 coughed into life and Franz Perschall climbed into the Komet. The steel cable was hooked on, Franz waved to us from the cockpit, and then the Bf 110 began pulling.

What exactly happened during the next two minutes was inexplicable. It was an absolutely calm and rather sultry day, yet the Komet appeared to stick firmly to the ground. The Bf 110 had become airborne long since, yet Perschall and his aircraft were still skipping along the grass, and for a moment it appeared that the steel cable was tugging in vain on its stubborn burden. Shortly before reaching the end of the field the Komet jerked off the ground, but Perschall appeared to be struggling laboriously to gain height. Ten . . . fifteen . . . twenty metres. The Komet staggered dangerously through the airscrew back-lash of its tug, then pulled up a little and followed the Bf 110 in a flat climb towards the horizon. We thought that it had settled down to a normal towed flight when, all of a sudden, it lost height rapidly and disappeared from our sight. The Bf 110 banked to starboard, and returned to the field on its own. Either Perschall had dropped the tow line or the cable had snapped.

We jumped in the starting vehicle and raced away in the direction of the spot that we assumed Perschall's Komet had landed, and, about two kilometres from the field, we found the aircraft among some scrub. At first sight the aircraft seemed to be virtually undamaged. Franz Perschall was still in the cockpit, draped unconscious over the control column with blood oozing from a deep wound in his face. More blood was spattered over the windscreen, and behind his shoulders were the tattered ends of his harness which had failed to take the strain. He was taken to hospital immediately, where he was found to have suffered two broken dorsal vertebrae, a double fracture of the skull and severe injuries to his jaw, as well as more superficial damage, and for several days he was to hover between life and death!

That was quite enough for a single *towed* flight, and enough for us, so we called it a day, and Karl Voy spent the rest of the afternoon explaining to Nelte, who had arrived in the meantime, and me the daily routine flying programme at Jesau.

Early next morning Nelte and I got busy with our

first towed flights, while Voy made a "sharp" take-off in one of the new Me 163Bs. As he took-off I had just dropped the towing cable at about four thousand metres above the field, and could easily follow every movement of the climbing Komet from my lofty seat. The take-off was beautifully clean and he climbed rapidly, shooting past like a bullet. Then his rocket began to smoke and an ominous black trail grew behind him. Then a drizzle of T-stoff began to fall away. The Komet faltered, and then Karl Voy's body flew clear. A few seconds later he was swinging merrily from his parachute.

As soon as I had landed, Nelte and I drove out at once to find Voy. A spiral of smoke from the crashed Komet led us a bone-shaking journey over rutted farm tracks, and we eventually found the pilot sitting on a tree stump and rubbing a sprained ankle. We had the greatest of difficulty in keeping straight faces, for poor Karl Voy's face was as black as a raven. Finally, unable to contain our mirth, we burst into shrieks of laughter.

"Damn it! Haven't either of you seen a man come down on a parachute before?" he shouted.

"We have, we have, Karl," I said, as I held a pocket mirror out to him, "but never a Negro!"

"Now I see it all," Karl Voy said. "Almost immediately after I had landed here, I saw two farm lads running towards me from over there, a big one and a little one. They looked just like Pat and Patachon*, and they got to within ten metres of me and stopped as though they had been rooted to the spot. Then they turned around and ran as fast as their legs could carry them. They must have thought that I was Lucifer himself!"

He stumbled around with a walking stick for a few days after his accident, but in no time at all Karl Voy was back with us testing out those Komets.

For a few weeks nothing more untoward occurred, if one discounts a few malfunctioning rocket motors.

---

*A famous pair of Danish film comedians of the 'thirties.

Otto Oertzen, who had joined us at Jesau as our Technical Officer and Engineer, was to be seen shaking his head over one or other of the temperamental brutes every day. There was a certain spot in the rear wall of the cockpit, just behind the pilot's head, of which Otto was obviously suspicious. Right behind this spot was a T-stoff fuel line joint and gasket, and it seemed that most of the awful smell came from here. The devil himself only knew where the fault lay and, unfortunately for us, Otto did not seem to be in his confidence.

One find morning Nelte jumped out of his plane screaming blue murder. Tears were streaming down his face from his red-rimmed eyes. He had just made a "sharp" start with half-full tanks and had managed a clean landing, but only just. He had been almost overcome by the stinging gas seeping into his cockpit, and he could barely see at all when he plonked his Komet down on the landing cross more by luck than judgment. Normally each of us tested one aircraft from start to finish. Then, if all was well, we declared it fit for operational use. On this particular day Nelte was due for leave starting after lunch, and he asked me, as a special favour, to make the final test flight in the particular aircraft that he had been testing.

"The motor is first class, Lieutenant, and I've already told them about that gasket, so you shouldn't get any smells in the cockpit." And then Nelte gaily departed.

Around 15.00 hours I climbed into the tanked-up Me 163B and made my final pre-flight checks. Otto stood beside me, intimating that he had given "this one" special attention and that it should purr like a Rolls-Royce.

"The motor of this one won't give you any trouble, Mano. Nothing can possibly go wrong, and those gaskets are as tight as a winged collar."

I pressed the starter, pushed the thrust lever to first stage, then stage two, checked the instruments and, with stage three I was away, the rocket motor roaring like a waterfall. The ASI needle crept round the dial rapidly. One hundred ... two hundred ...

three hundred kilometres per hour, and then I was airborne. The wheels broke away cleanly, I was across the boundary, and began pulling back on the stick. I could not have been more than two hundred metres off the ground when the fire-warning indicator began to climb with me. I pulled harder on the stick to gain as much altitude as possible, but the temperature was rising and the cockpit began to fill with that awful searing steam. At Jesau all R/T communications were in "clear", so I asked the controller if I was on fire.

"Nothing to see from down here," came the answer from below, but the temperature indicator was still climbing. When I passed the five thousand metre mark it had reached a frightening level, but the rocket was still going like a locomotive. The steam in the cockpit was getting progressively worse, and my eyes seemed to be on fire, but now the temperature gauge began to drop, finally returning to normal. I was still climbing flat out as I wanted to use up all my fuel as quickly as possible. I cut the rocket at eight thousand five hundred metres and, almost simultaneously, the steam in the cockpit thickened rapidly until it was as though I was sitting in the thickest fog. I could not even see my hands in front of my eyes, let alone the instrument panel.

"Cockpit fogged in!" I shouted over the R/T. "Looks as though I shall have to jump!"

"Wait till the cockpit clears and stay put if possible," came the laconic reply from below. Obviously Otto was more worried about his precious aircraft than about me.

I strained my ears for any abnormal sound but could hear nothing above the whistling slipstream. I put the nose down and pressed the Komet almost to its compressibility limitation, flashing down to six thousand metres and then pulling her up again almost to eight. No abnormal noise, but still that awful-smelling vapour in the cockpit. I pulled open the side panel built into the canopy, and the steam swirled about a little, giving me a clear downward view momentarily. I spotted the airfield and changed my course slightly, but by that time the cockpit was thick with the revolting fog again. I pushed a small piece of metal through the tiny panel in the canopy in an attempt to deflect some of the slipstream into the cockpit, but the air was still foggy and I couldn't see the altimeter clearly. At least, I could judge my altitude now, and I knew that if I jumped the Komet would probably fall into the middle of a sizeable village on the far side of the field. Apart from that, I had never used a parachute and felt that it was a little late in life for me to start.

"Don't bail out," came up from below, "your aircraft is flying normally!"

I began to get annoyed. It was all right for those characters on the ground. The aircraft was flying normally, indeed! If they could have seen as little as I could at that moment, they would perhaps have changed their minds. I tried to ease the burning sensation in my eyes and lifted my goggles, but the burning feeling intensified and so I pulled them over my eyes again. I suddenly caught a glimpse of my altimeter which read three thousand metres. More than enough to bail out in comfort. I began to feel dizzy, and black spots were dancing in front of my eyes. That could only mean the approach of unconsciousness and—the end ... I bit hard on my tongue and leaned as close as I could to the little side panel to gulp down some fresh air. Then I realized that I was still wearing my oxygen mask. Perhaps it was the mask that was making me dizzy. I ripped off the rubber mouthpiece and gulped in some air. It tasted like burned oil and sulphur. I had to cough and spit.

"Concentrate on your landing approach!" came a shout over the R/T. Then I suddenly realized that I was gliding away from the field. Then I had an idea. If I side-slipped, aiming my little window directly into the airflow ... ? It had the desired effect, for the fog thinned markedly and I could see once again. The landing cross was right beneath me by this time. I made a wide turn over a freshly ploughed field, and then, crunch! I hit the ground heavily. The Komet bounced several times and then the skid bit into the sparse grass, grated over some stones and gravel, and I was slowing down rapidly. To be on the safe side, I pulled the canopy release handle while the aircraft was still moving, punched my harness quick-release and stripped off my goggles. Then it happened! There was a blinding flash from the floor and a wave of searing heat struck my face! Instinctively, I pulled up my knees, planted my feet hard against the seat, and jumped for all I was worth. Maybe I landed on my head or possibly on all fours. All I could think of was putting as much space between me and that burning Messerschmitt as was possible in no time flat!

There was a bang behind me, and I ran like a hare for twenty or thirty metres, and then glanced over my shoulder. The Komet had come to a standstill and was steaming like a boiling kettle with the skid housing ripped wide open and half the cockpit blown away! By that time the fire tender, the ambulance and the starter truck were racing towards me at full speed, and, almost within seconds, jets of water were dousing the wreckage and Karl Voy and two of his mechanics were screaming at me: "Mano! Are you all right?"

My face and hands felt as though they were on fire, and the tears streaming down my face were stinging my cheeks like drops of acid, but before getting medical attention I wanted to take another look at the wrecked aircraft. The cockpit really was in a bad way. Both the finger-thick armour plates in the floor had been burst asunder like so much cardboard, their jagged edges turned upwards. Metal scraps were dangling here and there, every rubber connection had burned away, and the glass in all the instruments had been shattered by heat. The frontal armour plate was as black as soot, and had cracked in the middle like a piece of rotten timber. Pheeww! That time it had been close!

Once back in my quarters I had a look at myself in the mirror. Very pretty, I thought. My eyebrows and eyelashes had disappeared, together with a good third of my hair. I looked like a Tibetan monk! The doctor came in, daubed something on my face to ease the stinging, bandaged my head, and gave me a couple of pills, and in no time at all I was sound asleep.

Nelte came to visit me late that evening. They had probably told him about my narrow squeak as soon as he had returned from his pass, for he stood by my bed with guilt written all over his face. I could hardly speak, but all the same I could not resist the temptation to pull his leg.

"The motor is first class, Lieutenant," I mimicked. He made a face like a choir boy caught in the act of gulping a glass of holy wine.

"Hell, Lieutenant! If I had known that there was anything wrong with the crate I should never have asked you to fly the blasted thing!" he protested.

"Hell, Sergeant! If *I* had known I would never have let you visit your girl-friend!" I tried to laugh, but managed only a croak. "At least, I trust that she functioned a little better than that blasted plane did!"

The doctor grounded me for four days, and during that period Voy and Nelte flew almost continuously, endeavouring to keep abreast of the testing programme for the new Komets as they were delivered. Lamm had recovered from his crash, but a serious stomach disorder had put paid to his test flying, and it was to be months before Perschall would be back in circulation, and even then it was possible that he would be unable to continue flying the Komet. And so there were only the three of us, and we had to work like galley slaves. Take-off followed take-off, day in and day out, and there was no respite.

Apart from minor troubles, the rocket motors ran reasonably well, and under Otto's direction all the aluminum gaskets on fuel pipe lines were replaced by gaskets made of Buna*, and this appeared to be a

---

*Buna was the trade name for a synthetic rubber which, in some respects, was an improvement over real rubber.

major improvement. Flying was often sheer pleasure during those cloudless late summer days, and the early evening in particular was bliss. From altitudes sometimes as high as fifteen thousand metres, the view of the earth in the gathering dusk was indescribable, and the sky seemed afire with the setting sun.

In the meantime the Wittmundhafen squadron had been transferred to Brandis, and one day a Bf 110 landed at Jesau, carrying one of the old bunch in the shape of Sergeant Strasnicky. He had come to collect a new Me 163B and, of course, I pumped him dry, hungry for information. Nicky told me that they were now forming the first Komet Wing at Brandis under the command of a Captain Fulda—*a paratroop* officer! The task of the Wing would be the defence of the nearby Leuna fuel plant, so it was obvious that the original scheme of a belt of Komet bases stretching across the path of the daylight bombing formations had been abandoned. I blew my top again! Damn it all. Was I going to sit out the war here at Jesau without a single crack at one of the "heavies"? I roundly cursed Thaler, and asked Nicky: "Is that Thaler still at Zwischenahn?"

"Oh yes, Lieutenant. I nearly forgot to tell you. Thaler's days are numbered. Späte has been ordered to return to us as Geschwader Kommodore! We are known as Jagdgeschwader 400 now!"

My heart leaped with excitement at the news. Here was the chance that I had been waiting for. Späte wouldn't let me rusticate here! I went straight to my room and wrote a long letter to Späte, pouring out my feelings. If he had to form a Geschwader he would need personnel! I made Nicky swear that he would hand my letter to Späte the moment he arrived at Brandis, and I felt lighter of heart than at any time since being posted to Jesau.

Only two weeks after Strasnicky's visit I was summoned to the main office where a rather sour-faced Karl Voy told me that he had just had a phone call from Späte, and that I was to return to Bad Zwischenahn where I would receive posting orders to Brandis! Within twenty-four hours I was on my way, promising Nelte faithfully that I should do my best to wangle his transfer to Brandis as quickly as possible.

15

Revolutionary Armament

WHILE I HAD been languishing at Jesau a new development had been taking place at Brandis. For several
months Lieutenant Hachtel had been working his fingers to the bone in a vain attempt to turn the 30-mm.
MK 108 cannon into an effective weapon for use by the
Me 163B. It was not that the MK 108 was a bad weapon
as far as cannon go. On the contrary, it was basically
one of the most advanced weapons of its type to be
placed in production, but it jammed frequently and its
use in attacks on enemy bomber formations, bristling
with hundreds of large calibre machine-guns, dictated
tactics whose success was becoming increasingly pro-
blematical. It had become obvious that the Me 163Bs
principal advantage, that of speed, was lost when it
became necessary to jockey around for an ideal shooting angle. It was a problem that poor Hachtel could not
solve, and then, one day, a Doctor Langweiler turned
up at Brandis.

Few could have had a more inappropriate surname
than Doctor Langweiler* for he was a weapons special-

_____

Langeweile: weariness, boredom!

Panzerfaust

ist and the inventor of the notorious "Panzerfaust"*! The good doctor had arrived at Brandis for a very special reason—he had evolved a new and quite revolutionary armament for the Me 163B! He proposed to install a novel type of vertically-firing armament in the Komet's relatively thick wing roots. The idea was to fly beneath the enemy bomber formation and then fire the specially-designed shells in one salvo, these being triggered by light sensitive cells. In other words, the bombers would, in effect, destroy themselves as their shadows passing over the highly sensitive cells would act as a trigger! The idea was as simple as it was ingenious, but it had to be tested under operational conditions.

Langweiler was well prepared, having taken with him all the necessary equipment to Brandis, and, after a conference with the General of Fighters, he and Hachtel went to work. First of all, they built two of these vertical barrels into the wings of an Fw 190. Each barrel contained a 50-mm. high-explosive shell. The light sensitive cells were installed in the forward part of the wing, the necessary amplifier being housed in the

---

*The Panzerfaust was a one-man anti-tank weapon. Rocket-powered and having a hollow-charge explosive head, it was capable of penetrating the armour of practically every type of Allied tank, but a serious and dangerous drawback was its extremely short range—between thirty and fifty metres—and the "blow-back" flame.

fuselage itself. The barrels pointed upwards at a slightly oblique angle and also fanwise to achieve a certain spread and, in consequence, offer a greater chance of hitting the target. The explosive effect of a single shell was such that a hit on any part of a bomber would bring it down. Of course, some sort of a shadow was needed to activate the cells of the test aircraft, and eventually the idea of using two small barrage balloons was hit upon, these being fastened together by a piece of fabric about fifty metres in length and two metres in width. It was not anticipated that an experienced pilot would have any difficulty in flying under this "target".

The necessary preparations did not take long to complete, and one beautiful autumn morning, all personnel who could get away from their tasks stood around on the airfield to watch the first test run. The air was absolutely still, and the fabric was stretched taut between the two balloons. Hachtel made his final preflight checks and took-off in the Fw 190. In all honesty, few believed that this experiment could succeed. From the ground the "target" looked no larger than a piece of ribbon, and it was absurd to suppose that a fighter could plant a couple of shells through this from below! Hachtel made one trial run past the balloons, pulled up, went into a wide turn to bring him into position for his run, and then roared between the two balloon cables at some four hundred kilometres per hour. There was a puff of smoke as both shells fired, a bang, and then they were busily hauling in the balloons. When the winches creaked to a standstill all could see two beautiful holes slap in the centre of the fabric strip!

Everybody was dumbfounded by the astonishing success of the experiment, all except Doctor Langweiler, of course, and work was immediately initiated on further experiments. With two barrels in each wing, Hachtel scored three hits on his first and four hits on his second test flight, and with three barrels in each wing he hit the fabric five times out of a possible six, while with four barrels in each wing he holed the "target" in seven places! There appeared to be only one drawback to the scheme. As a result of the powerful pressure waves resulting from the simultaneous discharge of several barrels, the Plexiglas canopy of Hachtel's Fw 190 was badly cracked during the last two firing runs.

The aim of these experiments was to insert five of the shells in each wing of the Komet; and to distribute the tremendous muzzle pressure waves that would result when ten barrels fired together, it was proposed to load every consecutive pair of barrels with split-second delayed-action charges. Experiments with these charges were also one hundred per cent successful, and the full armament of ten shells was promptly built into the wings of an Me 163B. Only a few "empty" flights had been made with this machine when the Air Ministry stepped in and ordered the discontinuance of the use of the barrage balloons for the tests. The reason given was "Security". The chairborne warriors of the Air Ministry evidently believed that, as the balloons floated high in the sky, the experiments could be witnessed over a considerable distance. The alternative? Two high posts erected at one end of the field with the canvas "target" stretched between them. This would mean hedge-hopping the Komet to the target, but orders were orders!

The posts were duly erected, and next day Hachtel made his first take-off with a fully-armed Komet. As he did not need to climb very high, the fuel tanks were left half empty. Everything was now infinitely more difficult, for the posts stood only thirty metres apart, and the fabric strip was barely twenty metres from the ground! There was no room for a mistake or an error of judgment, but Hachtel had a steady hand, and forward view from the Komet was so good that he was sure that he could make a successful low-level firing run. Unfortunately, the day was not very clear, and patches of mist hung low over the field. Not low enough to cancel normal "sharp" take-offs and test flights, but for this experiment. . . .

Hachtel's Komet took-off cleanly, and went into a steep climb straightaway. Within a couple of minutes his rocket was silent, and he levelled off, banked steeply and began to dive towards the field with some nine hundred kilometres per hour on the clock, and then . . . calamity! They found him stretched out on the field, beside his badly damaged aircraft. He had cracked his spine and was unconscious. Later, when he regained consciousness in the hospital he told what had happened.

"I had those two posts slap in the centre of my gun sight," he said, "so I started to ease her out of the dive, intending to begin my low-level run some distance away. I switched on the sensitive cells and was about three hundred metres from the ground when, without any conceivable reason, there was a real thunderclap of an explosion. My head was flung back, slamming the head-rest, my goggles flew away and, suddenly, I felt as though I was sitting out in the open! I was dizzy for a split-second, and then I noticed that my canopy was gone and that the Messerschmitt was no longer on its course. I pulled up immediately, but I could hardly see anything at all. My eyes seemed to be full of muck and were pouring water. I could not see the field anymore and had only the vaguest idea of its position, so I went into a turn in the direction I thought the field to be. Next moment the field was slap beneath me, and I jerked the aircraft into a violent banking turn, came in too high, pulled up the nose, then pressed her down again, and slammed into the ground. I felt a tremendous stab of pain in my back, and had to clench my teeth to stay conscious. After it finished bouncing, the aircraft came to a standstill with a jerk, and I banged the harness release and jumped out, that being the last I remember!"

The accident was never explained satisfactorily. The only thing that was discovered during the subsequent investigation was the fact that all ten shells had gone off simultaneously—they had forgotten to load the specially-prepared delayed-action charges! His ten shells must have been triggered by the shadow thrown by a patch of mist.

All this had taken place before my arrival at Brandis, but I witnessed a demonstration of this novel arma-ment the day after my arrival. My old friend Fritz Kelb had taken over the test programme when Hachtel was

rendered hors de combat, and on the morning after I
had reported at Brandis, he took me to the big workshop hangar to show me an Me 163B with the new
armament. At first glance the aircraft looked very much
like any other Komet, but this specimen had five sheet-
steel tubes installed in a row in each wing root, about
seventy-five centimetres from the fuselage and protruding only two or three centimetres from the wing surface.
Each tube housed a thin-cased 50-mm. high explosive
shell which, he told me, was just about as effective as a
normal 88-mm. flak shell. In front of each row of tubes
was a light sensitive cell looking much like a blind eye.
These cells were activated by a button on the control
column, and from the amplifier in the fuselage a series
of wires led to each tube. Fritz's enthusiasm was such
that one could almost imagine that he had invented the
whole system, and when I expressed some doubts that
these gadgets really would function in the way that they
were intended, Fritz smiled, and replied: "You'd better
come out later on when I do a test and see what the
contraption will do!"

Two hours later he sat ready in the special Me
163B at the starting line. On the other side of the field
stood the two posts with the strip of fabric flapping
between them. Now that I could see it all with my own
eyes. I was even more sceptical of the scheme's feasibility.
I walked across to the target area and, together with a
few other interested spectators, took my place near the
posts. Fritz started up his rocket motor, roared along
the runway and was quickly airborne. Hardly two hundred metres up he went into a wide turn, and swung
back towards us like some flying reptile, tearing along
hardly ten metres from the ground. Then, just before
reaching the posts, he went down even lower, and then
howled past us like a demon. In a fraction of a second
he had swished between the posts, his rocket deafening
us, and, instantaneously, the fabric was ripped to shreds
by invisible shells. By the time our eyes had taken this
in, Fritz was far away, soaring into the sky.

I was speechless with amazement. If this ingenious
armament could be made to function under opera-

tional conditions and if enough Komets could be made available, then we might well be able to put an end to those deadly enemy daylight bombing attacks.

Fritz guided in to a clean landing, and I drove out to meet him. "Well, what did you think of that," he shouted, wearing an expression that he might have worn if he had brought down an elephant with one barrel.

"That was terrific," I said, "but can you do that every time?"

"That was my third go," Fritz told me. "My first try was a washout, the second time there were two holes in the fabric from four shells, and now this! We are still experimenting on the spread, but I believe that we are on the right track. I'll be making another test this afternoon."

I had to report my arrival to Späte at 09.30 hours, and so I made my way to the solid old house that accommodated the Geschwader Staff. A young lance-corporal directed me to a waiting room opposite Späte's office, and as I sat down I was rather surprised to hear Späte's voice so loud and harsh that it came clearly through the closed door. Späte was normally the mildest of men and rarely raised his voice, so he must really have been in a fury. Then the door opened and out came Toni Thaler, his face as white as a sheet. He saw me standing there, forced a smile and said: "Well, Mano, back from Jesau already?" I could hardly believe my ears. This was the first time in months that he had called me by my Christian name. Before I had a chance to reply, Späte appeared in the doorway and beckoned me into his office. We swapped a few reminiscences, I was told that I was to be attached to Geschwader Headquarters for special duties, and I learned that Thaler had been instructed to make his first "sharp" take-off with an Me 163B forthwith! Poor Toni. After taking things easy at Bad Zwischenahn all these months, and having avoided anything more exciting than a trip on the local train, he had to make a "sharp" take-off after all! Späte never demanded anything from anybody that he would not readily undertake himself, and it was only right that Toni should start catching up with the rest of us. Späte also informed me that First Lieutenant Medicus was to take on the task of looking after a new course of fledgling Komet pilots, and that a Japanese delegation was expected that afternoon to watch a demonstration, the task of ensuring that all arrangements went smoothly being delegated to me.

Our Japanese guests arrived on time, wearing their usual imperturbable smiles which they soon lost when we visited the workshop hangar where several rocket motors were blasting away on their test stands. One of the engines under test happened to be that installed in Fritz's aircraft, and Fritz himself sat in the cockpit, controlling the test run. When the familiar muffled bang announced the end of the fuel, and a cloud of white steam shot from the jet pipe, Fritz jumped from the cockpit and strolled over to the speechless Japanese.

"Wasn't that something!" he shouted to the Japanese who, still deafened, smiled politely, bowed from the waist, and stayed silent.

While the aircraft was being tanked up again, and prepared for the demonstration flight, we all walked slowly towards the take-off point, Fritz, constantly gesticulating and talking sixteen to the dozen, and our Japanese visitors politely laughing at jokes they obviously did not understand. When the aircraft was towed up, I helped Fritz into the cockpit, and gave him a hand in fastening his harness. Just before he closed the canopy he said: "Mano! Blue carnations are my favourites!"

"You'll have to make do with dandelions!" I shouted back at him through the little panel in the plexiglass. He made a good take-off and had climbed to about a hundred metres when the tailpipe spat out a few white balls of steam followed almost immediately by a thick trail of oily grey smoke from beneath the tail. The Komet was on fire. The smoking aircraft was now climbing somewhat erratically behind the airfield buildings, just over the fringes of the forest. I grabbed a pair of binoculars from one of the bewildered Japanese officers, and saw Fritz was doing his best to gain height. The canopy fell away, followed by a stream of T-stoff from the dumping valves, and then the aircraft pitched over towards the trees. I could see neither a body falling from the aircraft nor a parachute. Just a few metres above the trees something dark fell from the cockpit. Was it Fritz? I had a sudden glimpse of parachute shrouds, but almost as soon as I had seen them they had been swallowed by the trees.

I left the startled Japanese standing with their mouths wide open, raced to the starter truck and ordered the driver to go hell-for-leather towards the crash. The noise of Fritz's exploding Komet had long since died away by the time we raced through the airfield gates. There was no direct route to the spot where I imagined the aircraft to have crashed, and we had to take a roundabout way, soon leaving both ambulance and fire tender far behind. We left the road and bumped across fields, but a wide irrigation ditch forced us to

Kübelwagen

make another detour until we finally came to a small bridge spanning the ditch. By this time the ambulance and fire tender had caught up with us, but neither could negotiate the narrow bridge and were forced to turn around to find an alternative route. Our light VW-Kübelwagen could make it, however, and we raced on, bouncing across another field and through a small wood until we came within sight of the smoking remains of Fritz's aircraft. I jumped from the truck, shouting "Fritz!" at the top of my lungs, but there was no sign of him. The driver, who had run a little farther into the forest, came back with a piece of Fritz's parachute pack. It was not possible! Wherever that was found Fritz had to be as well! He could not possibly have escaped unscathed.

On the other side of the forest we found a house with several people gathered in front of it. We raced towards it, shouting: "Did you see the crash? Where's the pilot?"

"He's sitting inside!" someone shouted back. This was no time for silly jokes. But I was soon to discover that it was no joke. There was Fritz, smiling and wincing alternately as a pretty farm girl wound a moist bandage tightly around one of his ankles. At that moment, a second farm girl, even prettier than the other, came from the kitchen carrying a steaming pot of coffee. This was too incredible for words.

"Fritz! You really are the most amazing character that I have ever met!" I managed to stammer out as I fought to get my wind back. "Are you all right?"

He smiled, waved me towards a chair with a regal gesture, and said to one of the girls: "Miss Hilde—would you kindly bring another cup for our Mano here so that he can pull himself together. He really mustn't exert himself in this fashion!"

"I asked you if you are all right, Fritz!" I shouted.

"Well, yes and no!" he replied. "I lost my goggles on the way down, and I'm sure that I shall never get another pair to fit me so well. Then, of course, there is my foot. It may be sprained or perhaps I cracked it!"

It was only after the ambulance arrived, and a

young doctor had informed him solemnly that he had a bad sprain, and I had given the fire tender crew instructions for the salvaging of the wrecked Komet, that Fritz told us what had happened. It appeared that, realizing he would have to bail out, he had tried to jettison his cockpit canopy in the normal way, but the explosive bolts failed to function. He had released his harness and had struggled to force the "roof" off his back. Precious seconds had been wasted by the time he succeeded, and he had only just managed to bail out. From where I had stood on the airfield I must have been deceived by rising ground, for Fritz said that, at a guess, he was only some forty metres from the treetops when he tumbled from the cockpit. He fell alongside his burning aircraft, and would have hit the ground with a mighty bang if his 'chute had not snagged in the branches.

"I felt as though I had jumped off a church steeple clutching an umbrella," he said, "but in no time at all Hilde and Anneliese were there to give me a helping hand, and so I hobbled here. I've never pulled a ripcord so quickly as I did today, I can tell you! Oh well, you won't have to start gathering those dandelions for me!"

Once back at the airfield, his ankle was X-rayed, and the plates showed that he had a cracked bone. So our Fritz was to be out of action for a few weeks at least.

The air-raid sirens began wailing just as we finished celebrating Fritz's "birthday" that evening, and the flak was putting up a heavy barrage as we pulled on our leather jackets, left the mess and headed for our billets. Not a single point of light was visible anywhere except in the sky, but the beams of the searchlights silhouetted some of the larger buildings. Two of the long fingers of light crossed, holding a tiny silver-grey aircraft in their grasp. A third searchlight joined them, but the movements of the heavy bomber were clumsy and it was seemingly unable to escape from the brilliance in which it found itself. A line of short, stabbing flashes shot upwards from a near-by flak emplacement with a series of staccato cracks which reverberated against the sides of the hangars. Other flak batteries joined in, adding their quota of steel to the fusillade screaming up towards the point where the searchlight beams imprisoned the intruder. The exploding shells seemed to creep closer and closer to the fleeing aircraft. Shrapnel clipped the ground occasionally around us, but we were impervious to all but the drama being played out above us. Several other searchlights had now added their light to that of the others.

"Someone ought to climb up there in an Me 163 and put an end to this cat-and-mouse game," one of our number muttered. "Trying to land in the dark you'd spread yourself in small pieces around the countryside!"

A shell seemed to burst right alongside the bomber, but it continued on serenely, then faltered, and something seemed to fall away from the brightly lit machine. Then a parachute blossomed a little way below the bomber and slowly swayed out of the arc of light. The bomber banked steeply to port, and then there was a flash, followed by a glowing fireball, and the searchlights were once again probing across the night sky, searching out another victim.

16

Our Numbers Dwindle

LATE NEXT AFTERNOON I found time to visit Fritz Kelb. I was not a little surprised when I opened his door to find him limping around the room instead of lying in bed.

"What the heck do you think you are doing, Fritz?"

"I'm taking walking exercises. I can't just lay about here. I get all sorts of damned silly ideas lying in bed and twiddling my thumbs, and anyway, if I hang about here Franz Rösle will take over my test flying tomorrow."

"So what?" I replied. "Let him take over for a few days and you get back between the blankets and rest that cracked bone."

I finally persuaded him to get back into bed, but Fritz was feeling thoroughly morbid.

"This bed is not doing me any good at all, Mano," he said. "I begin to think that I may be losing my nerve. I have been lying here, thinking to myself that we all have only so much luck and once we have used it up . . ." he snapped his fingers. "We make one or two 'sharp' starts every day. Everything is fine, then you get a real stinker but you manage to get down in one piece. The same thing happens again but when you have fun and games like I had yesterday, you realize that you are beginning to push your luck! The day must come when all the cards are stacked against you. You know, Mano, at times I feel as though I am hanging over an abyss from a rope and my fingers are gradually slipping. In fact, I am not at all sure that our whole country is not hanging from a rope now, and the question is how long will it be before we have to let go?"

Fritz's depression was infectious, and I began to wonder deep down if he was not right. But gradually I managed to tear him away from his gloomy thoughts, and he was soon his usual gay self again. As I was about to leave, he said: "Oh, that reminds me, Mano. Franz Medicus wants to talk to you. He's having some trouble with his brood of chicks."

I telephoned through to Franz Medicus's room, and he told me that he would come straight over to see me.

He certainly looked worried when he arrived, and I asked him what the matter was.

"Jo mei, Mano," he started in his Bavarian dialect, "maybe these youngsters haven't got the guts for the Komet, but six or seven of my bunch put in for transfers after witnessing Fritz's performance yesterday, and at this rate I shall not have any left in a week."

"How many are there now?" I enquired.

"Right now there are twenty-eight, but tomorrow . . . ? I thought perhaps you would be willing to give them a little pep talk. You can do that sort of thing better than I can, and perhaps it will help to stiffen their backbones."

"O.K., Franz. Tell them to be in the breakfast hall at 08.30 hours tomorrow. I'll have finished my business with Späte by that time, and Franze Rösle will probably be making a 'sharp' take-off around about 09.00 hours, so it will be a good time to ask them squarely who wants to stay and who wants out."

The problem of our "rising generation" of Komet pilots was a ticklish one. To compel them to fly the Me 163 was senseless. Nobody could fly such an aircraft and survive if he had an insurmountable fear of it. We all knew that, and so did Späte. He had never forced anybody to fly the Komet—you either did it of your own free will or you left with no recriminations. On the other hand, the problem of recruiting young pilots was becoming increasingly disturbing. Very soon we would need hundreds of new pilots for the Komet if this revolutionary fighter was to be reasonably successful and effective on operations.

Next morning at 08.30 hours sharp, I stood in the breakfast hall facing the twenty-eight rocket fighter trainees. These twenty-eight young pilots had volunteered to fly the Me 163B on operations. Admittedly, some of them had been pushed a little, and many of them now deeply regretted their daring. What could I tell them? Almost every one of the recruits had come to Brandis straight from the elementary gliding school at Gelnhausen where flying had been little less than sheer pleasure. Could I now tell them that they were binding themselves to a unit in which their chances of staying alive for any length of time were little better than one in a hundred?

I decided to make it short and to the point. I told them in no uncertain terms what they could expect if they stayed with the Komet, and I certainly did not glamourize the situation. I watched the twenty-eight faces in front of me, noting by their expressions how very different their reactions were, and by the time I had finished my "pep talk" I had a pretty good idea of how many were likely to stay and how many were likely to leave for safer pastures. In the event, my guess was to prove pretty close to the mark.

Franz Rösle stood by his aircraft at the take-off point, swapping crude jokes with his mechanics, as, together with Franz Medicus, I left the hall and walked across the field. Rösle's repertoire of indelicate stories was quite notorious. He had no respect for anybody or anything, and he had no respect for the Komet. He would climb into his cockpit with the same light-hearted audacity that he would use to pick up a girl. In appearance he closely resembled Adolf Galland, our General of Fighters, moustache and all. I sometimes believed that Franz's indifference was all an act to hide a deep-set self-consciousness, but as his laugh echoed across

the airfield like a piece of sheet metal being dragged
over a bed of nails, it was hard to believe that he, too,
suffered fears and anxieties. His friendship was uncon-
ditional, and he spared no efforts to help others when
the need arose.

Franz Rösle climbed into the cockpit, as ebullient
as ever. There was some last-minute repartee with one
of the mechanics, the cockpit canopy was pulled into
place and locked, then he had pressed the starter, his
rocket had screamed into life, and he was climbing
away from the field like an arrow. He drew wide spirals
above our heads, and I thought to myself that this was
just the sort of demonstration that was needed to in-
spire our fledglings who seemed to have lost all their
apprehension as Franz flashed past us only a few metres from the ground. He pulled the Komet up steeply,
turned into an elegant landing approach, and touched
down, skidding along the ground perfectly balanced.
As the Komet was slowing down, there was a searing
blast of flame from the cockpit, and clouds of steam
swirled around the fuselage! It seemed that Franz flew
rather than jumped from the cockpit, hitting the ground
with a tremendous impact. There was no vehicle to
carry us to the scene of the accident and, for once,
there was no sign of either fire tender or ambulance. I
shouted at the man standing aghast at the start telephone:
"Get an ambulance here, but quick!"

And then, with the others I was running towards
the steaming aircraft. The fire tender raced past us just
as we approached the spot, and the scene could not
have horrified me more had I found poor Franz laying
dead at my feet! Franz stood there screaming and groaning alternately, and kept shouting for somebody to
pour water over his body! But his face . . . Oh God! I
was never to forget his face! There was no skin, no
eyebrows, no hair, only a ragged stubble of what had
been his proud moustache! I was nearly overcome by
nausea, swallowed hard and clenched my teeth. There
was still no sign of the ambulance! Two of us took his
arms and led him gently towards the fire tender and we
finally got him to the sick bay. Two of the nursing

orderlies fainted immediately they saw his poor, mutilated face, and another ran from the room to be sick. All this time Franz was groaning and cursing, and then the doctor arrived and we left him.

Franz Medicus and I walked silently towards the Operations Post. I could see nothing but Franz Rösle's terribly mutilated face. I prayed that his eyes had escaped injury even if his face had gone! Franz's face, always laughing and grinning . . . and now! "He'd be better off dead," I muttered to Medicus, but he didn't reply, and took leave of me at the Operations Post to return to his sadly discomfited fledglings.

When I reported to Späte and Olejnik that Rösle's face had been almost totally burned away by T-stoff, they only pursed their lips in silence. Then, after a brief reflection, Späte said: "When First Lieutenant Rösle is fit enough to be interrogated, get the whole story from him, Ziegler, and then prepare a written report."

As he dismissed me the air-raid sirens began to howl. I jumped on my motor-cycle and rode straight to the starting point where Schubert, Ryll, Bott and Glogner were seated in their aircraft at "Immediate Readiness", listening intently to situation reports over the R/T. I walked over to Bott's aircraft and climbed the small ladder.

"They're coming directly towards us now," he said, after a moment or two. "Yes, it will be Leipzig or Berlin. Now they're changing course a little. No, they are back on course and it looks like Leipzig."

The sky above was azure, and only over Leipzig and the adjoining complex of the Leuna Works was there a brown industrial haze. And then, high above but still far away a phalanx of contrails appeared, moving towards us at a snail's pace. It was as though some immense hand was dragging a white paintbrush across the clear blue bowl of sky.

"This is going to be hell! They've really got it in for us *this* time," said Kurt, a young mechanic from Berlin, with a hint of panic in his voice.

"We're off!" shouted Bott, as he pulled down and locked his canopy, and gave Kurt a signal to operate

the starter. Almost simultaneously, the other three starters began turning over, and less than a minute later,
Schubert was roaring across the field, followed closely
by Ryll. Another minute and Bott and Glogner had
taken off, leaving their jettisoned wheels dancing drunkenly across the field. High in the sky, the bomber stream
began to change course slightly. Leipzig had evidently
been a feint, but not I could see the first contrails from
our Komets. Evidently Schubert and Ryll. Their delicate,
silvery threads were heading straight for the bombers.
Anxious minutes passed, and then the first of the Mes-
serschmitts whistled low across the field, pulled up again,
and then came in to land. It was Glogner, the last of
our quartette of Komets to get airborne. He was boiling
with rage, his rocket having cut at seven thousand metres,
leaving him no alternative but to return without a crack
at the bombers. Soon afterwards Bott landed. His motor was smoking, his cockpit was full of steam, and tears
were pouring down his face. A T-stoff pipe had developed a leak, and he too had been forced to break off
the pursuit.

    Schubert and Ryll came in to land almost simul-
taneously. Schubert shot across the field at six hundred
metres, waggling his wings furiously. A kill! We soon
learned that he had intercepted a Fortress and shot off
its starboard inner engine, but he had had to break
away before he could observe it "going in". Ryll had
been bounced by two escorting fighters and, as his
rocket motor had already cut, he could do nothing but
go into a steep dive to shake them off. In the meantime,
the second Rotte* had taken off with Husser and
Eisenmann at the controls. The wind had changed, but
there was no time to rearrange the direction of take-
off. The Komets had to make do with a tail wind! Alert
followed alert, with reports of new bomber formations
coming in every few minutes, although none of them
could be seen from our airfield, apart from the tail end

---

*A Rotte comprised two aircraft, the standard basic unit of
Luftwaffe fighter squadrons. Two Rotten comprised a Schwarm,
and three or four Schwärme formed a squadron of staffel.

of the last formation which was being pursued by Husser and Eisenmann. Three other Me 163Bs stood at "immediate readiness" at the starting point, with Glogner, Strasnicky and Rolly in the cockpits, and while they were awaiting take-off orders. Husser and Eisenmann returned, but as neither waggled his wings we assumed that they had had no luck.

Husser made his landing approach first and came in against the take-off arrow which was still pointing in the wrong direction. We could not see his approach clearly as our view was partially obscured, but it was obvious that he was much too high as he crossed the airfield perimeter. It looked as though Husser was trying to press his Komet to the ground by force, and the Messerschmitt hit the field with tremendous force, bounced back into the air, and then shot towards us at terrific speed. It did not touch down again until it had reached our end of the field—by that time it was too late. Husser's Komet raced over the airfield perimeter, crashed through some bushes and turned over. There was no explosion, and I had just seen a few of the ground personnel leap into the starter truck to drive to the scene of the crash when somebody swung me around and pointed to Eisenmann's Komet. It had just completed its landing approach but, again, it was much too high. All at once, Eisenmann put the aircraft into a vicious sideslip and began losing altitude fast.

"Get out, man!" somebody shouted, but it was already too late for Eisenmann to bail out. The Komet touched the ground, leaped back into the air and skated towards us for a couple of seconds, then half-rolled on its back and touched the ground with its starboard wingtip. In a flash the Komet became a fantastic catherine wheel which flew straight at us, turning over and over, showering burning debris in every direction. I threw myself to the ground and saw Glogner and Rolly leaping from their aircraft as the burning mass tore past us, coming to rest about a hundred and fifty metres farther on. Wreckage was strewn all around, and we found Eisenmann dead but still strapped in his seat alongside the remains of the fuselage.

Beyond the airfield perimeter, four of our mechanics had, meanwhile, reached Husser's Komet and, despite the probability of an explosion any second, were endeavouring to force open the smashed cockpit canopy. Ignoring the ominous hiss of escaping T-stoff, they wrenched and pulled until they finally succeeded in wresting Husser from the wreckage, lifting him, groaning in agony, on to a stretcher.

But there was no time to think on these tragic events at that moment. I helped Glogner back into the cockpit of his aircraft and saw Strasnicky and Rolly preparing for a hurried take-off. Another bomber formation had been reported heading straight for our field, and this time there was apparently no doubt about it. Orders came from the Command Post to take cover immediately. It was already too late for the Komets to take off, and Glogner, Nicky and Rolly jumped from their aircraft once more. Almost over our field the enemy formation suddenly changed course, and so, for the third time, they scrambled back into their cockpits and started taking-off.

Rolly was first off and made a clean start, but he had hardly attained an altitude of fifty metres when a white cloud of steam belched from his tailpipe and the rocket motor quit! Rolly struggled desperately to gain height, and just about managed a hundred metres when he bailed out. But his 'chute did not open in time . . . ! Glogner's young face was drained of all colour as he received his take-off order half-a-minute later. He shot across the field with his rocket roaring full blast, but for once everything went well, and Glogner's Komet was soon lost to sight. Strasnicky, Ryll and Schubert followed shortly afterwards, taking off on their second interception of the day.

Nicky was the first to return, and it seems that, in the excitement of taking-off and climbing full pelt to interception altitude, he had forgotten to decrease his thrust when levelling out of the climb and had experienced some violent compressibility effects. Before he could regain full control of his aircraft he had lost three thousand metres in altitude, and there was nothing for it but to return to base. Glogner came back soon afterwards as did Schubert, both empty handed, but Ryll had clobbered a Fortress, shooting it down in flames with his first burst. The day's balance sheet: Two "kills", two of our pilots dead and three of the Komets written off— and oily black clouds of smoke hanging over Leipzig were reflecting hungry red flames in the evening dusk.

That evening in the mess we were torn between our mourning for two good comrades, Eisenmann and Rolly, who had been members of our "bunch" from the very first day that Test-Commando 16 had been formed, and our desire to celebrate Schubert's and Ryll's "kills". And so we celebrated, emptying a tidy few bottles of Dutch gin, of which there was no shortage as Böhner's squadron had brought an immense supply of it from Venlo.

In the mess I bumped into Franz Medicus. "Well, what are your fledglings doing now?" I asked.

He smiled bitterly, shrugged his shoulders, and said: "Only seven of 'em left now. All the rest have asked to be taken off the course!"

That was another item to be added to the debit side of the day's ledger of our activities, although I doubt if I would have stayed after witnessing the day's performance had I been one of those young trainees. No, one couldn't blame them at all.

During the course of the evening I visited the sick bay with a glass of gin each for Fritz and Franz Rösle. Fritz was cursing his luck and swearing that he would be flying again on the morrow, come what may, but poor Franz was in no condition to do any swearing. His whole head was swathed in bandages in which were cut three small holes for his eyes and mouth. He was still in very severe pain, and could hardly move his lips without suffering acute agony. He accepted the glass of gin with alacrity, however, and after he had emptied it through a straw, he whispered: "It looks as though boozing is to be my only pleasure in future, Mano!"

"Don't talk like that, Franz," I replied. "They can do miracles these days, and in no time you will be as good as new." He attempted to shake his head, but the pain forced him to lay back on his pillow again.

"Listen, Mano," he finally said, his voice near to hysteria, "they want to take me to a hospital in Halle or Leipzig tomorrow. For heaven's sake, try to get them to let me stay here."

I promised him that I would do what I could, and then went back to the mess, thoroughly depressed. I could not help comparing the present crowd with the old familiar "bunch", now no more. Many new faces had appeared in the mess during the formation of Jagdgeschwader 400, some pleasant, some not so pleasant; some friendly, some unfriendly. The most comical face, however, was undoubtedly that of an Austrian Major named Bazilla, a man not without merit but so Austrian in his ways that he might have fallen out of old Franz-Joseph's waistcoat pocket. Bazilla played a violin, badly but persistently. He was a bundle of nerves and chain-smoked sixty or more cigarettes a day. In fact, I do not recall having ever seen him without a cigarette between his fingers, except, of course, when he was torturing the strings of his beloved violin. Exactly how Bazilla had come to find himself among us I was never to learn, but he was there, and our mess was the richer for the presence of this original character. As I entered the mess he was making a valiant start with "Gipsy Melodies" from Sarasate, not that the composer would have recognised Bazilla's rendering. Count Schweinitz, our Silesian nobleman of the purest blood, rose from where he was sitting between Medicus and Bott, and shouted: "Damn it all, Bazilla! Why don't you chuck that wet fiddle away once and for all. Your playing gives me chronic indigestion!"

It was not a particularly witty remark, but the term "wet fiddle" had been coined and stuck straightaway. From that moment on, anything that did not function properly was a "wet fiddle".

It must have been around midnight that Späte walked into the mess. When he spotted me, he came across, and said: "A new job for you, Ziegler. From tomorrow on you will take over the training of our recruits, together with First Lieutenant Niemeyer, and, later on, the reserve squadrons as well—that is, of course, when the reserve Geschwader is formed."

"Does that mean that there will be more operational bases for the Komet, Major?" I asked, for I could not see how we could accommodate more squadrons at Brandis, which was already overcrowded. One day the Yanks were going to lay a carpet of bombs on us that would send the whole outfit up in smoke. But it seemed that I had touched upon a GeKado matter, because Späte replied rather brusquely, "That's not your worry, Ziegler"—and turned away.

The following days brought some really lousy weather, freeing us from daylight bombing raids. But we couldn't make a single take-off either. And then, one morning, the sun was shining brilliantly again, and the smoke from the tall Leuna chimneys was climbing almost vertically into the blue sky. We now had no time to lose, and everybody who could, wanted to, or had to fly was out at the starting point bright and early. The operational squadrons had nine Me 163Bs at combat readiness, and their pilots, Nicky, Bott, Mohr, Schubert, Ryll, Reukauf, Zimmermann, Andreas, and Jupp Mühlstroh, were stretched out on the grass.

Niemeyer and I began our scheduled training programme—one "sharp" and two towed Me 163B take-offs and a towed Me 163A take-off each—and I made a demonstration flight to give our charges some confidence. After I had landed and the Me 163B had been tanked up again, I sent off the first of my initiates, a blond youngster named Ernst from Lower Saxonia. He was one of the few who simply could not get behind the controls of the Komet quickly enough, and under his eager hands the rocket motor functioned perfectly, the wheels dropped away at the right time, and his soaring Komet had soon disappeared from my view.

"Did you let them fill her up to the brim?"

I turned around and found Fritz Kelb standing behind me. Up and about again, although still limping a little, Fritz had been busying himself around the

vertically-armed test Me 163B which was being prepared for another trial, but he had apparently watched
Ernst's first "sharp" take-off. He knew as well as I did
that a pupil was not permitted to fly with a full load of
fuel on his first "sharp" take-off, and he also knew that
if anything happened to Ernst I would find myself well
and truly "on the carpet".

"You guessed it, Fritz," I replied.

"But why?"

"Because I think that it does not make the slightest
difference and, besides, it saves time and an unneces-
sary training start. If we tank them up fully from the
outset I can get through that much quicker. What difference if they do roll along another hundred metres
or so at take-off? They still come in to land under the
same conditions however much fuel they take-off with!"

"You're right, Mano, but don't forget the altitude.
They are not used to ten or twelve thousand metres
yet, and they have to return home just the same."

Fritz was perfectly correct, of course, and I shouldn't
have sent off any pupil with full tanks on his first
"sharp" start, but I was so sure that nothing could
happen to Ernst. I knew him too well. I was still trying
to convince myself how well I knew Ernst as minute
after minute ticked by without any sign of the Komet
returning! Another minute passed like an hour, and
then Fritz spoke up again: "Well, I reckon that you
don't have to wait any longer, Mano."

"Shut up, Fritz!" I replied ferociously, but deep
down inside I knew that he was right. Ernst had not
returned, and according to my watch twenty minutes
had passed since he had taken-off. No, he would not
come back now. As I was thinking these gloomy thoughts,
our portable telephone rang shrilly, and a lance-corporal
shouted my name. It proved to be our operations room.
They had just received a call from Leipzig-Mokkau
informing them that an Me 163B had made an emergency landing there and had exploded on running into
a bomb crater. The pilot, a young man named Ernst,
was safe and sound.

How on earth had he got away with it? How did he

get to Mokkau in any case? The distance between Mokkau and Brandis was only short. Wild ideas chased through my mind, and I had to discover for myself what had happened, so I asked Niemeyer to take over my group as well as his own, called a car and set off for Mokkau. In no time I was standing on the edge of the bomb crater that had the wrecked Komet strewn around its inside. It had blown up with tremendous force, there could be no doubt, and yet Ernst stood beside me, very much alive and in one piece. Then Ernst told me his story:—

"Everything was fine up to seven or eight thousand feet, but then, all of a sudden, my oxygen supply failed! My mask felt as though it had a plug in it, so I ripped it off and dived for the safety altitude—four thousand metres. In the meantime, I had lost sight of our airfield, and could see only Mokkau beneath me. As my time was running out, I made up my mind to risk coming down on Mokkau. I made a good landing approach, and it was then that I saw those bomb craters. I just had time to find a narrow strip of grassy field, touched down clean, and skidded along beautifully for a few hundred metres, but then this crater appeared in front of me. I simply could not avoid it! I was still travelling about sixty kilometres per hour, and so I held tight and in we went. I must have damaged the canopy release somehow, for I could not wrench it off no matter how I tried. At that moment, a young flak auxiliary came running towards me with an axe in her hands. She chopped the canopy to bits and I scrambled out. By that time the fire tender and the ambulance had arrived on the spot, and perhaps a dozen or so flak people as well. I shouted at them to take cover straightaway, grabbed the girl, and rolled with her into the next crater, and then came the bang!"

That was Ernst's story—short and painless. Almost unbelievable but true, nevertheless, and the only casualty was Ernst's heart, for his saviour was a decidedly attractive young creature!

*   *   *

That evening we "old-timers" sat around in Bott's room. There was Fritz Kelb, Hans Bott, Franz Rösle, still covered in bandages, Jupp Mühlstroh, Franz Medicus, "Bubi" Glogner, Günther Andreas, Nicky Strasnicky, and the few others—all that remained of the old "bunch", and my closest friends. Rumours were going around that the reserve Geschwader had already been formed and was to be transferred far to the East, to more peaceful pastures. If the rumours were true it meant another farewell for me, although we all knew from experience that such rumours could be totally false. This rumour, though, was to be borne out in fact all too soon.

We talked idly about this and that—flying, women, the progress of the war. Subconsciously we must all have known that, for Germany, the war was lost, but none of us would consciously admit it and, instead, we dreamed of a thousand or more Komets ready to take-off the instant an intruding formation was sighted to knock them for six. We even talked of our plans for after the war, and one of the most popular was the idea of organizing flying shows with the Komet. Of course, it was nothing more than a roseate pipe-dream for we knew that one of us would "buy it" every few days and we would soon run out of pilots for our show. It may sound strange, perhaps, but in our own way we loved the Komet. Perhaps it would be more truthful to say that we were fascinated by her in the way that one can be fascinated by a woman that takes all the money from your pockets every day and then deceives you every night. Of course, few of the newcomers felt the same way about the Komet as we did. They were blasé about the dangers at first, but after they had witnessed a few "sharp" starts with perhaps an explosion thrown in for good measure, the wind was soon taken out of their sails and, more often than not, they promptly headed for pastures new. One such was our good Major Bazilla—our "wet fiddle".

It happened the next morning, as a matter of fact, when he was to make his first "sharp" take-off. The Komet stood at the starting point, tanks half full according to regulations and, for the last time, I explained to Bazilla the purpose of every handle, lever, knob and button in the cockpit, and once more took him through all the emergency procedures. As I gave him my last admonitions he was running nervously around the aircraft, puffing great clouds of smoke from a cigarette shaking between his lips. He was moving so rapidly that I found it difficult to keep pace with him.

"Once more then, Major, Sir," I said. "After jumping the blocks, keep the control stick in normal position. When you feel that you have enough lift, ease back a little on the stick and wait for it to steady. Take care that she does not swing sideways. If she does, correct with your rudder immediately. After you unstick don't press her like an ordinary aircraft. Let her rise on her own. Remember that you mustn't drop your wheels from too great a height. Drop them between five and ten metres and then trim her a little more nose heavy. Keep your eyes on the pressure gauges, and if during take-off the pressure drops seventeen or eighteen atü, switch off the motor and roll her out on the field. After you have crossed the perimeter and your air speed indicator shows some eight hundred kilometres per hour, pull her up steadily to five or six thousand metres. The rocket will fade out somewhere around this altitude, and when that happens pull back your thrust lever and glide down to two thousand metres, making a few turns and banks on the way. If you like, you can also make a few short dives, but don't lose sight of the field. Start preparing for your landing approach from two thousand metres, and take her in the last landing turn at between eight hundred and a thousand metres over the field, and then come down. You will be perfectly all right."

Bazilla's hands trembled as he dropped the remains of his cigarette and climbed into the Komet's cockpit. He promptly got his seat belts entangled and then could not find the seat adjustment handle. Then he searched vainly for the starting button. If I had had my way I should have asked him to climb out again there and then. In his former Geschwader Bazilla had been a highly successful fighter pilot, and I could not very well expose him unless he backed down himself. Finally, the canopy snapped shut and Bazilla was on his own. He seemed to calm down and pressed the starter button bravely, sitting there like Richard the Lion Heart on his charger. There was a jerk, and with the third thrust stage, the Messerschmitt jumped the third thrust stage, the Messerschmitt jumped the blocks and rolled away.

Everything *seemed* to be going all right, the Komet rolling across the field as straight as a die, the motor functioning perfectly. Then, all of a sudden, the rocket faded out! One moment it was roaring away healthily and the next it was silent, and clouds of white steam were pouring from the tailpipe. The Komet left the runway in a wide turn, and rolled away over the grass. Our hearts were in our mouths. If the Messerschmitt decided to dig its nose into the soft ground and turn turtle, the good Major would be gone in a flash—literally!

Hardly daring to breath, we watched the Komet trundle along, jolting and rocking over the uneven ground, gradually slowing down. Finally, it came to a standstill and, instantaneously, the canopy flew off and Bazilla bounded from the cockpit and ran for all he was worth away from the aircraft! We gave chase and finally caught up with the Major a few hundred yards from the control tower. He stood facing us, shaking with a mixture of fury and fear, another cigarette already between his nicotine-stained fingers. To my questions as to what had happened to warrant this remarkable performance, Bazilla replied in his inimitable Austrian dialect: "The engine failed. The bloody thing lost fifty revs right after the start! It's impossible—no sane man can fly that bastard! It's sheer suicide!"

"But Major," I replied with all the patience I could muster, "I told you distinctly that you should cut the motor *only* if the revs dropped to seventeen hundred. When they swing a little between twenty-one and twenty-four hundred it doesn't matter a damn."

"Jo, d'you believe that I'm going to hang around until the bloody thing blows up?" he roared.

"On the contrary, Sir," I said, trying to keep my face straight, "I thought that you were introducing a new style in rocket hara-kiri! What you did was just about the surest way to get an express ticket to Hades!"

The major looked a little non-plussed, and stuttered: "Well, you can see that I'm still alive."

That was about the last straw! "You can damned well thank your lucky stars and the good nature of the aircraft that you played about with like a child," I replied passionately. But I could see that the Major had just about had enough, and he was going to pull rank on me.

"Perhaps I am the best judge of that, Lieutenant Ziegler," he said haughtily. "I know exactly what I'm doing. Give me a decent aircraft and I'll make a 'sharp' start this afternoon."

"That's out of the question, Major," I said. "Five towed starts and a few standing rocket runs first. I shall not let you touch a sharp Komet before."

He was now beside himself with fury. "In that case, you can keep your bloody death-trap. I'll go back to my old squadron," he shouted. "In any case, I am getting bored to tears here," he added as an afterthought.

Our "wet fiddle" packed his case the same day and we never set eyes on him again.

17

The End Draws Near

THE GIANT operational airfield at Udetfeld in Eastern Silesia was allocated to us as our rocket fighter training field, and we were transferred there with two "school" squadrons, Adolf Niemeyer taking over the 13th Squadron and I the 14th. Our pupils, for the most part young and enthusiastic fellows, had come straight from the glider training school in Gelnhausen where they had been trained up to Stummel-Habicht standard for fast skid-down landings. Our training programme remained much the same as before—towed and "sharp" starts with the Me 163A followed by towed starts with empty and water-ballasted Me 163Bs and, finally, three "sharp" starts with the Me 163B. The pupil was then considered to be trained to operational standard, and in this way we were supposed to turn out ninety trained pilots per squadron per month.

This was plain wishful thinking on the part of the chairborne warriors who had formulated the programme and stipulated the pilot output. Apart from the fact that the training procedure was much too protracted to achieve the demands made upon us, we were short of virtually everything. Therefore, on my own initiative and responsibility, I decided to start my pupils off straightaway on a water-ballasted Me 163B, followed by a "sharp" take-off. The scheme was an immediate success and progressed without accidents, a very considerable amount of time being saved. But even that did not help much for, suddenly, we would be short of T-stoff for a whole week, or something else was lacking which prevented the continuation of the training programme. At such times we had to keep the pupils occupied with theoretical lessons, some of value and some quite valueless. One of the lessons that fell within the former category was taught by "Bebs" Bob, a young Major who, a highly successful fighter pilot by trade, had been posted to Udetfeld to test a new type of gyroscopic gunsight which had been specially designed for fast aircraft, such as the Me 163B and the Me 262. As his test flights with the new sight were limited by the fuel shortage, he spent his time instructing the pupils in correct sighting methods with high-speed aircraft. In itself it was a vital subject, but it was eventually to become so much wasted effort when it became increasingly evident that our pupils would never see any action in which they could make use of their knowledge.

Adolf Niemeyer quickly tired of the periods of inactivity which lasted for days on end, and soon found a way to add zest to his life. He had discovered that we shared Udetfeld with a special Commando engaged in experimenting with the new air-to-air rocket missiles, and it did not take Adolf long to obtain the necessary authorization from the Geschwader Headquarters to "borrow" twenty-four R4M rocket missiles and fit these beneath the wings of an Me 163A. Nobody knew what effect the addition of these missiles would have on the airflow beneath the Messerschmitt's wings, but Adolf, who approached everything like a bull at a gate, was too impatient to undertake a towed start, and ordered the tanks to be filled and made a "sharp" start straight away. The Me 163A proved amenable to the modification, and climbed away steeply, rockets and all. Adolf made a perfect landing and, for nearly four weeks afterwards, conducted firing trials with the R4M rockets, proving the possibilities of this remarkable armament.

To my knowledge, this was a world première—the world's first rocket-propelled aircraft to be fitted with rocket-propelled armament.

And then, one day, the Russians were virtually knocking on our front door! Hurriedly, we pulled back to the West as their armoured spearheads crunched their way towards us. With my squadron I left for Sprottau where we were soon pitching our tents, with a frightfully worried station commander, who until that moment had enjoyed a peaceful existence, hovering around us. I managed to arrange a few "sharp" starts for my pupils, but in no time at all we were once more falling back in front of the Russian armour and, early in January 1945, by a somewhat roundabout route, we found ourselves once more at Brandis.

Brandis—destined to become the graveyard of the Komet—was one of the very few airfields still left intact and undamaged by bombs inside beleaguered Germany. It was to see the last chapter written in the epic of the Me 163. The skies above Brandis and Leipzig had become a hell, and the earth beneath a mass of craters, rubble and fire-spitting guns. The choking, acrid smoke from the holocaust that had been a city climbed almost uninterruptedly into the sky, which seemed to be continuously full of bombers pouring white-hot iron into the gaping wounds below. The enemy escort fighters twirled and cavorted like shining toys, and the anti-aircraft barrage provided a continual cacophony.

Our operations became more difficult and more dangerous with each passing day. When one of us managed a clean take-off and the rocket motor functioned efficiently, a hundred dangers lurked in the skies during that period when the helpless Me 163B was coming in to land, for the enemy now knew of the rocket fighter's Achilles' heel. Amazingly, our airfield was *still* undamaged. The wide field *should* have been churned up by a carpet of bombs long since, the runways *should* have been pitted with craters and the hangars raised to the ground months before, yet by some fantastic quirk of fate Brandis had survived unscathed. Many of our Komets stood ready at the starting points, available for immediate interception sorties, and those not at "instant readiness" were in the large maintenance hangars, being checked over by tired mechanics. In the forests around the airfield perimeter stood more than a hundred brand new Me 163Bs, as yet unflown and all carefully camouflaged. But the invisible ghost of the imminent and inescapable end determined and shaped our days. We all knew that time was running out and Death's bony fingers were tapping on our shoulders. We had lost the war. Who could now doubt it? Why fight on and get ourselves killed as well? Yet, day after day we sat in our cockpits, some of us dozing fitfully over our controls, jerking back to life and reality as the R/T crackled in our ears with take-off orders, and we were once more roaring down the runway in pairs or, at the most, threes to attack those seemingly endless trains of bombers with their countless escort fighters jinking around them protectively. Then back again with a Mustang waiting until the rocket fighter was helpless in its final landing approach!

P-51 Mustang

Fritz Kelb's Me 163B stood in the maintenance hangar. It had flown its last operational sortie, and there were one hundred and forty-six holes in its fuselage and wings! But not one bullet had found its billet in Fritz who, somehow, had brought his sorely dam-

aged mount into a perfect landing. Schubert had chalked
up his third "kill", and most of the others had recorded
their first or second. Up till that time all too few enemy
bombers had found their approach or homeward journey barred by the Komet, but we had knocked down a
round dozen, and a few days later was to come the real
storm.

Formation after formation of the enemy roared
over Brandis, and Schubert and Bott were the first pair
to push their starter buttons. Their turbine starters
hummed, their rockets roared and they were gathering
speed across the field. Suddenly, the diamond wave
pattern of Schubert's rocket motor disappeared in a
flash of flame and cut out completely. The Komet had
already reached about two hundred kilometres per hour,
and Schubert had no chance of stopping the aircraft
before it reached the end of the runway! We watched
Schubert begin a wide turn, pass over the runway
boundary, his aircraft rocking from side to side over
the uneven ground. A wingtip touched the ground and
spun the Komet around. The tail swung upwards, the
aircraft toppled over and, instantaneously, there came
the crack of an explosion and the aircraft had disappeared in a boiling cloud of flame!

Bott had got away to a perfect take-off and had
already disappeared from sight. We prayed that he had
not seen Schubert's fatal crash. Nicky and Bollenrath
went up as the next section, followed by another pair of
Komets. Then there were only two more Me 163Bs
standing at the starting point, those of Günther Andreas and "Bubi" Glogner. Alongside Andreas's aircraft
stood the chief of its ground crew, Corporal Ferdi
Schmidt, another of those who had been with us from
the very beginning, and remembered the trials and
tribulations of Bad Zwischenahn, with its first trium-
phant rocket flights and our first sacrifices. Ferdi was
looking at the Komet as though he had built it with his
own hands, anxiously yet proudly. Ferdi was typical of
the members of our ground crews—his cap was always
set at a jaunty, non-regulation angle on his head, his
trousers were too wide, but his heart was in the right

place, torn between aircraft and pilot. He would never
let us down, and he would sacrifice night after night of
badly-needed sleep to ensure that his charge functioned
with perfection.

Ferdi bustled around the Komet, testing the undercarriage pin once more, examining the rudder travel,
satisfying himself that nothing had escaped his eye.
Then came the take-off order, and Andreas and Glogner
were roaring down the runway. The sky was swarming
with enemy fighters and bombers, their contrails in
broad phalanxes boring across the sky, some of the
fighters drawing a delicate filigree as they dived and
soared around their charges. Minutes passed and the
first of our fighters began to return. Ryll had a "kill"
but Bott and Glogner had been unlucky. Nicky came
in. He too had a "kill", and then we saw another Me
163B coming in high above the field. From that distance we couldn't see if it was Bollenrath's or Andreas's
machine, but we *could* see the Mustang that had followed it down and was now rapidly closing to firing
range! We stood there helplessly, watching the drama
unfold. The Mustang pulled nearer and nearer to the
unsuspecting victim, and then, like a buzzard swooping
on a dove, it pounced. We could not even see the
tracers; only a little smoke, a flash and it was all over.
Bits and pieces fluttered down to the ground, and
among them was Bollenrath!

Andreas got back to Brandis—but by car! He had
passed the bomber formation at six thousand metres
but had continued his climb to ten thousand before
turning in for his firing run. He had set his sights on a
Fortress that was straggling a little behind his fellows,
lined up carefully, and opened fire. But almost simultaneously splinters were whirling past his head, blood
spurted from a wound over his right eye, and his cannon jammed! He broke away immediately and, expecting his aircraft to burst into flames at any moment,
tried to jettison his canopy. It was stuck firmly. His
speed had dropped to two hundred and fifty kilometres
per hour and he had unbuckled his seat harness to
enable him to press against the canopy with his elbows

and finally jerked it free. Busy as he had been with these troubles, Andreas had not spotted a Mustang creeping stealthily up from behind. A moment later the American announced his presence by raking the Komet with his sextette of 0.5-in. machine guns. After a few violent and uncontrollable antics, the Komet went into an almost vertical dive, screaming like a phantom, and this involuntary dive probably saved Andreas's life for, by the time he once more got his aircraft under control, the Mustang had gone, and he could take to his parachute in peace.

We had long since learned not to take death too seriously, and although we mourned our comrades, we felt that, in some respects, they might have been fortunate. We were inured to danger, having lived with it for so long, and our earlier fears had evaporated. All of us felt that we no longer had anything to lose and it is not so difficult to be courageous once that state of mind had been reached. But even among those only recently trained on the Komet there were no dodgers.

Among these newer Komet pilots was a Sergeant Klein, a splendid young fellow with blond hair and a handsome face. I had taught him from his first towed starts at Udetfeld and had watched him make his first "sharp" starts at Sprottau. He was as bold and as fearless as a young lion, and during his very first powered flight he had dived on the field "right from the top", and had swept across hardly ten metres from the ground at tremendous speed, pulling up sharply like a veteran at the other side of the field, cavorting about briefly as though he had been born in the Komet, and then coming in for as perfect a landing as I had ever seen. His third and fourth "sharp" starts were also his first operational flights from Brandis, and after the latter we saw him spiralling down followed closely by a Mustang. He must have known that the American was on his tail for he continually tightened his turns. In no time they were down to less than a thousand metres, but the Mustang pilot, sure of the continuous power of his engine, could afford to bide his time, particularly as the flak could not fire for fear of hitting young Herbert

Klein. On the other hand, poor Klein could not keep gliding indefinitely, and finally the Mustang pilot opened up. We saw Klein's aircraft buck slightly, and then glide steadily down behind the trees.

They carried the Sergeant back on a stretcher. At first sight he appeared to be uninjured, but he was dead. The Me 163B had come down in a large field and had apparently made a normal landing, suffering virtually no damage. It was unbelievable. They had found Klein dead in his seat, the control column gripped tightly by his stiffening fingers. There was a single small hole in the back of his head—the one bullet that had penetrated his seat armour.

18

Volunteers for Suicide

EARLY ONE morning, Geschwader Headquarters ordered the pilots of both Komet Wings to assemble, and Captain Fulda, the commanding officer of the 1st Wing, began to read an order signed by Reichsmarshal Goering. After a long preamble about the distress being suffered by our Fatherland, our wives and our children exposed increasingly to the mercy of enemy bombers, and our duty to sacrifice ourselves if needs be in their defence and for the victory of Germany, the order came to the point—it called for volunteers from amongst us prepared to fly ramming attacks against enemy bombers in Messerschmitt 109s. The Führer himself, it seemed, was anxiously awaiting a report as to the number of pilots willing to volunteer for this suicidal task. Nobody was forced to go. Only volunteers were wanted, and as he finished reading the order, Captain Fulda, a married man with three children, announced that he had already forwarded his name as the first of the volunteers.

None of the pilots had more than a few minutes to make up their minds about volunteering for this mission; a mission that would clearly demand their most precious possession—their lives. We had often talked amongst ourselves about the possibility of ramming enemy bombers, and there were known cases where a pilot *had* succeeded in saving his own life after knocking down a bomber in this way. But it was patently obvious that an appalling risk such as this could only be taken once, or twice at the most. To expect to survive a third such attack was ridiculous. So the decision facing these young pilots was clear-cut. They had to decide if they had the courage to die for the "cause". Whether this "cause" could be saved by their sacrifice was beside the point. The "cause" and "final victory" had become a religion—one either believed in it unquestioningly, or . . . !

And then the volunteers stepped forward: Bott, Glogner, Löscher, and a few more—eight men in all. They were told that the new ramming squadrons to which they would be posted were to be formed at Stendal.

As it happened, I knew nothing of all this until late the same afternoon when I returned from a short visit to the Air Ministry in Berlin. A mighty blanket of dank grey fog lay over the ground, and the bare, black trees groped upwards to disappear into nothingness a few feet from the ground. A half-frozen sentry stood at the gates, peering suspiciously at me through the gloom until he recognized me, and the whole airfield seemed deserted as I walked to our barrack block. I carried a few things that I had purchased in Berlin to my room, and then went to look for the others, knocking in turn on Bott's, Rösle's, Kelb's, and, finally, Schweinitz's door, but none of them was in. This was strange. It was rather early for them to have gone to the mess. But on a day like this. . . . I soon found them. Those who were not in the mess were in the adjoining wing where some of us had billets, and for the most part they were either blind drunk or nearly so! Schweinitz lay on somebody's bed, singing and groaning alternately, and when he saw me enter, he wiped his chin with one of his shirt cuffs and shouted: "Mano! Hey, Mano! Here you are at last! Fetch your guitar and join our gay, gay party! Come and get thoroughly, repulsively drunk, Mano! Nothing matters anymore!"

"Shut up, Count," Sturm intervened, although he

was anything but sober himself, simultaneously throwing a wet towel which hit Schweinitz slap in the face. Sturm was a blade of a rare kind. A hardy reserve captain, he had been a pupil in my training squadron at Udetfeld. He was an excellent pilot in general and a superb glider pilot in particular. Whenever he had the chance he would grab one of the Stummel-Habichts to practise low-level aerobatics, and only a few weeks had passed since he had smashed one of these into the ground coming out of a low-level loop. Those who drove out to the other side of the field where they could see a heap of matchwood marking the spot where the Stummel-Habicht and the earth had collided expected to find the smashed body of the pilot as well. They were intensely surprised to meet a happy and smiling Captain Sturm who, very much alive, simply shook the odd pieces of the glider from his body, like a dog shakes water from his fur after a swim, and walked away. He was a man in which were combined sturdiness and absolute dependability. When Schweinitz took up his demand for my guitar once more, Sturm just said, sternly: "Shut up once and for all, Count, otherwise you'll soon find yourself in no condition to sing." Then turning to me, he said: "Don't take any notice of him, Mano. He's as tight as a drum! In fact, we've all been boozing since midday."

Fritz Kelb, Hans Bott and a few of the others had reached the unpleasant stage of semi-soberness that remained unaffected however much more they drank, and finally I learned from them of the happenings of that morning.

"Well," I said finally to Fritz Kelb—"have you volunteered by any chance?"

"No bloody fear!" replied Fritz vociferously, and nobody could ever have accused *him* of cowardice.

"Eight of us have volunteered," said Bott quietly, and then listed them, placing his own name at the end of the list. Eight splendid fellows volunteering to commit suicide. It was unbelievable. What did they think that we could gain by such methods? We were just tickling the enemy with feathers while he was replying with tons of fire and steel. It was lunacy.

"You must be completely mad," I shouted. "Do you think that you can stop this damned Juggernaut with a measly handful of Messerschmitt 109s? If you ram a hundred, a thousand, they'll still keep coming on. It's like spitting into an ant-hill."

"Don't get excited, Mano," Bott replied quietly. "Whether we blow ourselves to kingdom come here or bash ourselves to pieces against the tail of one of those Fortresses it will all be the same in the end."

We were all silent for a while, and I thought furiously. Something totally incomprehensible seemed to have happened while I had been away. This desire to die was idiotic. O.K. So we couldn't change the course of the war with our handful of Komets at Brandis, nor could we alter things by throwing ourselves away in suicidal ramming attacks. It was so irrational. It was the concept of a madman. We had five-and-a-half years of war behind us. Surely we had not come to this. Thousands of Reichsmarks had been spent on our training and now we were asked to throw ourselves at our enemies, not to kill *or* be killed, but to kill *and* be killed!

Eventually I sent one of the orderlies to get my guitar, and gradually our spirits began to lighten. We swapped the latest spicy stories, sang, and emptied glass after glass. Our would-be suicides became as gay as if they had not a care in the world for, in truth, soon they wouldn't have—at least, not in *this* world. They began to discuss eagerly the best methods of ramming attack in much the same way as they might have discussed means of gaining the favours of the local girls a year or two back.

"Slam the wing of the 109 across the Fortress's tailplane—the 109s tough and will probably stand up to that treatment, and if you're really lucky you will still be able to land the crate."

"No, tear off the Fortress's rudder with your airscrew," said another.

"Damn it all, man! That would call for some really fancy flying, and remember you'll be sailing through a curtain of lead. No, a sharp, knife-edge dive to tear off an aileron, that's the answer."

And so the argument went back and forth, and the more they drank, the more idiotic became their schemes for cutting the Fortresses out of the sky. And all the time the hands of the clock moved round the dial pitilessly.

The next morning, loaded down with suitcases and kitbags, our eight valiant heroes climbed aboard a lorry that stood dejectedly in the fog outside the airfield gates. Their gay shouts seemed hollow to my ears, and I thought to myself as they sat themselves on the hard wooden benches that they were not to have a comfortable ride even to meet Death. Loscher stuck his head through a rent in the canvas covering, and shouted: "After the first one, you'll get a postcard. Perhaps from Heaven . . . well, from Hell certainly!"

And then the rickety old lorry jerked away into the fog. Those of us who remained walked sadly back to the mess. Nobody said a word, and only one filled his empty glass. In the half light of early morning the mess presented as depressing a spectacle as one could find anywhere outside a graveyard. Stale tobacco smoke hung heavily in the air, small puddles of spilled wine lay on the tables among the dirty glasses, and as I plucked a few sad notes on my guitar, a fist crashed on one of the tables. The tough Captain Sturm let go with such a stream of invective that the glasses jumped about on the tables. And then his head fell forward on the table and his shoulders heaved.

19

And So Dies JG 400

SSOME HOURS later the sun was shining brightly from a cloudless sky. I sat down to fight a minor war with a heap of the innumerable forms that I am sure would still have called for attention had I been queueing at the gates of Hades. Fritz Kelb phoned to tell me that two of the Me 163Bs that had been undergoing overhaul had to be flight-tested, and suggested that I might care to take one of them. I didn't need to be asked twice, and grabbed my flying kit and headed for the starting point.

I am sure that Fritz must have been in much the same mood as myself. The light-hearted way in which our comrades had left in the early hours had no doubt had some effect, and our earlier depression had evaporated. For once I did not feel that tightening of the chest which previously had preceded every "sharp" take-off in the Komet, and we both climbed nimbly into the cockpits of our Me 163Bs as if they were no more than harmless rowing boats on a lake, pressed the starter buttons and, within a few seconds of each other, were rolling down the runway, rapidly gathering speed.

Fritz's rocket motor seemed to be giving more power than mine as he pulled away from me rapidly during the take-off run, but I dropped my wheels as soon as I could and soon caught up with him on the climb. Wingtip to wingtip we shot upwards, the sky turning bluer and bluer. At seven thousand metres Fritz's rocket cut out, but I continued climbing for a little while until my rocket also cut. I banked and put the nose of my aircraft down, and there was Fritz, drawing circles a good thousand metres below me. I dived towards him, he broke away, and we began a wild chase, diving and banking around each other like playful seagulls. The Komet was really a superlative aeroplane when flown "empty", and the I.A.S. swung between two hundred and five and nine hundred and fifty kilometres per hour as we climbed and dived in turn, feeling like carefree swallows in that clear, clean air, but all good things had to come to an end, and I put the nose of my Komet down to gather speed, sailing past Fritz, rocking my wings to let him know that I was going in for a landing.

I saw him turning in, following my approach from higher up, and then I began to concentrate on my landing. I was still a little too high and so I lowered the landing flaps earlier than usual. Hardly had I done so when my aircraft flipped hard over to one side, picked up speed and went into a vicious banking dive. What the hell was the matter? I raised my landing flaps, levelled off and lowered them again . . . and then the warning light went on. One of my landing flaps was stuck!

Time was running out and I had to think of something quickly. I could no longer approach the field in a straight line. If I did I would drop slap into the bushes somewhere beyond the perimeter, and that would mean flipping over on my back and, in all probability, the final curtain. I banked to port away from the field, my idea being to make another approach diagonally. I banked once more to starboard, gliding close along the airfield perimeter, lower and lower. If I could just scrape over the hedge. . . . Then I saw a stationary goods wagon on the railway line next to the field, and it was slap in my path! I pressed the nose of the aircraft down fractionally to pick up my last bit of speed and then pulled up smartly to leapfrog the wagon. At that moment my hair stood on end. Hidden behind that long wagon were three T-stoff tank cars. They were right in front of me and I was barely twenty metres from them. It seemed impossible that I could leapfrog these as well—I was already much too low. I made a split-second decision, pulling hard on the stick, aiming for a small gap between the tanks. The fuselage of my aircraft slipped through the gap, the wings just brushing the tops of the tanks, and then the Komet dropped to the ground like a ton of bricks.

I felt no pain. I lay there for what seemed an age but, in reality could have been no more than a few seconds, and then felt the heavy R/T set and half the instrument panel pressing on my legs. Blood was dripping down my face, and I swallowed a broken tooth. I heaved on the R/T set and pushed it aside. I could not believe that I had survived this crash with no more than a cut face, a bruise or two and some broken teeth. Carefully I ran my hands over my legs, moved my feet a little, but they seemed to be in excellent shape. I had been so busy examining myself that I had not noticed the fire tender and ambulance racing towards me. With squealing brakes, they came to a standstill beside the aircraft, and technicians, medical attendants and firemen were suddenly scrambling all over the place. Two were laboriously forcing open my jammed canopy and had, in no time, helped me to the ground.

"Come on, Sir. That thing can still blow up. It's stinking quite indecently," one of them shouted to me. I hadn't even given the possibility of the aircraft blowing up a solitary thought until that moment. But the powerful jets of water from the fire tender were already at work, and I was soon seated comfortably in the ambulance on my way to the sick bay. After a thorough examination the doctor gave it as his opinion that I had merely suffered a slightly strained backbone, ordering me to rest as much as possible for the next few days!

Black days now began to trouble us. The air over our base became an exericse ground for American fighters which seemed to amuse themselves by laying in wait for returning Me 163s, shooting them down like lame ducks as they made their landing approaches. Our star was truly in the descent. Ryll fell a victim to an American fighter in this fashion after his third "kill", and one day we waited in vain for our happy-go-lucky Nicky to return.

In the midst of it all, there was *one* bright moment—the return of Bott, Löscher, and the six other volunteers for ramming attacks. They arrived back at Brandis from Stendal without having achieved anything. A superb farce could have been written around their experiences. Upon their arrival at Stendal, the volunteers had had to suffer many long and solemn speeches intended to explain to them that their superb self-sacrifice could mean a turning point in the course of the war. And then they had had every possible good thing lavished upon them to prepare them for this flight. After a few days they learned that the few miserable attempts at aerial ramming already made had proved complete failures, that there were not enough aircraft to go round, and, in any case, there was no fuel with which to fly them! The whole thing thus became a comedy but, who knows, the idea may have gained a few favours for some of the chairborne warriors around Hermann Goering.

From the operational viewpoint, Brandis was now silent. Our losses had been so catastrophic that we were forbidden to intercept bomber formations enjoying fighter escort, this order reaching us from top level. We were only permitted to take-off and intercept unescorted reconnaissance aircraft, and so we kept our eyes peeled for such day after day. Apart from myself—I had to wear a special corset to remind me of my fun and games with the T-stoff tank cars—everyone of our pilots who still survived was fit for combat duty. Even Franz Rösle had his face back in some sort of shape and had grown his moustache once more.

Despite this lack of activity, our pilots sat in their cockpits at take-off readiness each day. Sooner or later a reconnaissance aircraft was bound to show up, and

P-38 Lightning

then. . . . At last, one evening, a couple of photographic
Lightnings were reported approaching our field. It was
shortly before sundown, and the take-offs had to be
made immediately if anything was to be achieved. A
few minutes after we had received the R/T report, a
pair of delicate contrails appeared high in the sky,
golden in the late evening sunlight. Our visitors! We
estimated that the contrails were at an altitude somewhere between eight and nine thousand metres. Bott
and Rösle pressed their starter buttons and were soon
shooting steeply upwards, and by that time the contrails
had made the Lightnings an easily recognizable target
in the violet evening sky.

On reaching eight thousand metres, Rösle found himself only two hundred metres away from the Lightnings, and keeping his eyes on the enemy, he levelled off. A few seconds later one of the Lightnings was squarely in his gunsight. Then, without any warning, his Komet jerked up almost vertically, shook violently, and then went into a wild dive, the control column being yanked out of Rösle's hands. A quick glance at his airspeed indicator provided the answer to this erratic performance—it stood at one thousand and fifty kilometres per hour! Rösle had inadvertently exceeded the Komet's compressibility limitations. Bott, who had been flying just behind him, fared no better. He had maintained the same speed as Rösle and, before he had realized what was happening, his aircraft had gone through the same box of tricks. Of course, they had both reacted almost instantaneously by slamming back the thrust lever, but these unwanted manoeuvres had already lost them so much altitude that both Lightnings had put too much distance between themselves and their intended attackers for a further attempt to intercept them to be made. They were practically bubbling with rage when they landed, both certain that the Lightnings would have been sitting ducks but for their bad luck.

The next morning "Bubi" Glogner enjoyed better luck. An R.A.F. Mosquito, probably sent to take photographs of the previous night's bombing damage, was reported approaching almost at the crack of dawn. It was not a very clear morning, with large clumps of cloud hanging between heaven and earth, but Glogner was soon climbing away like a fiery arrow. He lost sight of the Mosquito, and when he had reached fourteen thousand metres he had almost decided to give up and turn back to base when he spotted the Mosquito once more far below him. The Englishman did not seem to have noticed the Komet, and was flying sedately on, apparently unaware that there was anything else in the sky. Glogner put his aircraft into a dive and overhauled the Mosquito rapidly, but just before he could get the intruder into his sights, the Mosquito made a sharp turn and went into a steep dive. Glogner had his hands full, trying to line the rapidly moving target in his gunsight. He put the nose of the Komet down sharply, pulled up from a near-vertical dive and found himself sitting almost on the Mosquito's tail. After three short bursts the Mosquito's port engine belched fire and smoke. Large pieces broke away and both crew members bailed out of the stricken aircraft.

Glogner broke away, diving into a large cloud—at least, he thought it was a large cloud as he couldn't see a thing outside his cockpit. Then he realized that it was not a cloud at all. The inside of his canopy was coated with a thick layer of white frost. Rubbing had no effect whatsoever, and as fast as he scraped a strip away it closed over again. He knew the score only too well, as he scratched away desperately. If he couldn't see from the cockpit he could never find the field and might just as well close his eyes there and then and wait for the bang. His A.S.I. still showed eight hundred kilometres per hour, but the altimeter was unwinding fast. Finally, he succeeded in scratching a small peephole through which he could see the ground between the towering cloud masses. There was a large built-up area, obviously Leipzig, but of Brandis airfield there was no sign. Within seconds the peephole had iced over again. Perhaps it would soften if he flew lower into warmer air he thought, but he had to keep his diving angle shallow as he would otherwise be left with too little time to find the field. He slowed down to about two hundred kilometres per hour, stalled once, righted the aircraft, and then managed to scratch another peephole. Then, to his joy, he saw part of the Brandis runway between the banks of cloud.

He put the nose of his Komet straight down, diving through a large cloud, but by this time the air was becoming warmer and the layer of ice in his cockpit began to soften. He scratched another hole which began to spread, but his altimeter now read one thousand metres and he was still diving in thick cloud without a glimpse of the ground. Eight hundred . . . six hundred . . . four hundred metres, and then the cloud began to

thin and, suddenly, the airfield was spread out before
him. He made a U-turn over neighbouring Zeidlitz to
cut down his speed, made his approach, more by guess-
work than anything else, touched down and, after two
or three tremendous bounds into the air, came safely to
a standstill. Even after coming to a standstill the nose of
the Me 163B was covered completely by a layer of thick
ice, and the cockpit canopy was not much better.

Glogner's flight was destined to be one of the last
"sharp" starts from Brandis and, if I remember correctly,
his was also the last but one of our "kills". Our time was
running out rapidly, and the air was rife with rumour.
Our aircraft were to be destroyed and we were to be
given rifles and take our places in the front line. . . .
We were to be retrained on Me 262s and the Me 163Bs
were to be scrapped. . . . These and other reports from
"well-informed sources" circulated continuously until
we began to take no notice of them as each story became wilder than the one it replaced. We carried on
just as before. A number of Me 163Bs stood ready at
the take-off point each morning, some sort of training
of new Komet pilots continued, and the workshops
were as busily overhauling Komets as before. In spite
of strict orders which forbade any such flight, Fritz
Kelb took off, attacked and shot down a bomber with
his vertically-armed Me 163B, and it was during one of
these days that Franz Rösle made his last flight in the
Komet; a flight that ended unbelievably quickly.

The whole performance took place so near the
field and so low that we could witness in detail the
whole sad event. The starting procedure, the roll-out
and take-off, were perfectly normal, and the Me 163B
lifted off easily and, right after dropping its wheels,
began to climb away steeply. It had only attained an
altitude of about a hundred metres when the rocket cut
out. Franz pulled the aircraft up as high as he could,
"pulled the plug" to dump his fuel, and then turned
back to the airfield. Watching his aircraft from the
ground, we saw a cloud of grey smoke belch from the
tailpipe—an ominous sign suggesting that it was time

Franz baled out. Franz evidently also thought that it was time to get out, but it would seem that the emergency canopy release failed to operate. He evidently undid his harness and pushed against the canopy with both hands. It gave way at last but did not fall away from the aircraft. Franz wriggled through the opening sideways but, as he did so, the Komet went into a knife-edge turn, and the canopy slammed down, trapping his legs.

By that time, the aircraft, with Franz hanging from the cockpit by his legs, was barely a hundred and fifty metres above the field, and we could see all too clearly his desperate struggle to release his legs from the grip of the canopy's sharp edge. Fortunately, Franz was wearing a pair of large felt flying boots and, with a mighty heave, he succeeded in pulling one of his feet free from its boot, and then, planting this firmly against the fuselage side, managed to liberate his other foot. By the time he fell free, the aircraft was at an altitude of a little more than a hundred metres. Franz pulled on his ripcord but he was too low. We watched him tumbling through the air and then, just before he hit the ground, his chute jerked open.

We ran across the field where we found Franz unconscious beneath the folds of his chute. X-ray photographs revealed a fracture lumbar vertebra, necessitating a plaster of paris corset which led him to give vent to some really choice language when he finally came to in the sick bay. We sympathized with him for he had only just taken off the last of the dressings from his head and face, and now this.

Franz Rösle's short but highly eventful flight almost brought to an end the story of the Me 163B Komet. The wildest of rumours were now hardening into sharp facts, and by that time the Me 262 had gained its first successes as a defensive fighter. The most successful of the Luftwaffe's fighter pilots had been gathered together to form that famous unit* where

---

*This unit, Jagverband 44, was formed in January 1945 at Brandenburg-Briest under Generalleutnant Adolf Galland, and

many a Geschwader Commodore and men whose names were household words, such as Galland, Steinhoff, Lützow, and many others flew as simple pilots in sections and flights. The circle of steel was closing in on Germany, and this was little more than a dramatic finale. Our Commodore, too, went to that last fighter unit, and took with him some of our most experienced pilots. Only a few survived, and Fritz Kelb, who had been one of our best, failed to return from his last operational flight on the last day of the war.

And so died Jagdgeschwader 400 and, with it, the Me 163B Komet. We had failed to achieve our aim, but the fame of this fantastic warplane was not to rest on her successes. The number of victory stripes that bedecked her fuselage were small, but she had opened a new era in flying. A mettlesome creature as gentle as a dove one moment and a fiend at others, she was unique.

---

more than half of its forty to fifty pilots were highly experienced and included ten holders of the coveted Ritterkreuz. The unit was finally over-run by American armour on May 3, 1945, at Salzburg-Maxglan.

Appendix

The Origins of the Messerschmitt Me 163

THE STORY OF the Messerschmitt Me 163 really began one day in November 1925, when a young aircraft designer, Alexander Lippisch, took over the technical direction of the research institute of the Rhön-Rositten Company for Glider Flying at Wasserkuppe. Lippisch was a fanatical advocate of the tailless configuration for aircraft, and had carried out a large number of preliminary experiments in this field, building and testing numerous models. He designed and built his first successful full-scale glider of all-wing configuration in 1926, and flown for the first time in 1927 by "Bubi" Nehring, it was dubbed the Storch (Stork)—an appropriate enough name as during that year Lippisch's son Hangwind was born.

Trials with the Storch were conducted by Nehring and Fritz Stamer, various improvements being incorporated progressively, until, early in 1929, by which time the glider was known as the Storch III, the test programme was taken over by Günther Groenhoff, then Germany's most successful glider pilot. Following the completion of gliding trials, an 8 h.p. two-cylinder air-cooled DKW engine was fitted, this driving a small pusher airscrew. As the Storch V, the aircraft made its first powered flight on September 17, 1929. Its flying

weight of 551 pounds gave a power loading of 6.9
lb./h.p. During a flight from Wasserkuppe to Kreuzberg
and back, the Storch flew at an average speed of 78
m.p.h., and so good were its characteristics that it was
decided to demonstrate the aircraft at Tempelhof, Berlin.
Officials from the Ministry of State Transport and the
German Aviation Experimental Establishment were
unimpressed. Insofar as they were concerned the tailless configuration offered no advantage whatsoever.

Among the spectators was Frau Herrman Köhl,
and her husband, who had not been present at Tempelhof, requested that another demonstration be arranged.
Köhl was convinced of the future of tailless aircraft,
and the demonstration took place at the Böllenfalltor
auxiliary airfield, near Darmstadt. The weather was
extremely poor but, finally, Groenhoff decided to chance
it, and took-off. The Storch climbed away from the
field with ease but, after completing one circuit, was
suddenly hit by a strong downward gust, and Groenhoff
made a crash landing. Despite the accident, Köhl gave
his financial support to the tune of RM 4,200, and this
sum was used to create the Delta I.

The new aircraft featured marked sweepback on
the leading edges of the wing, the trailing edges being
straight, and thus, in planform it bore some similarity
to the Greek letter △ (delta). All aircraft of broadly similar planform were subsequently to be known as Deltas.
The Delta I was completed as a glider in the summer of
1930, and after initial flight trials to determine the
characteristics of the new aircraft, a 30 h.p. Bristol
Cherub engine was fitted. In its powered form, the
Delta I flew for the first time shortly before Whitsun
of 1931, a speed of 90 m.p.h. being attained. A demonstration of this aircraft induced the Horten brothers,
Reimar and Walter*, to take an interest in aircraft of
tailless configuration.

---

*Reimar and Walter Horten were later to be responsible for
the design of the Ho IX tailless twin-jet fighter-bomber which
was to have been built in quantity as the Go 229 by the
Gothaer Waggonfabrik.

Once again it was decided to give a demonstration at Tempelhof but, unfortunately, engine trouble developed during the ferry flight to Berlin. The engine failed twice on the way to Tempelhof, and the third time immediately over the airfield. Groenhoff succeeded in making a successful landing, and it was then ascertained that the main bearings had "eaten in" solid. Fortunately, a new engine was acquired and the demonstration took place on October 25, 1931, as planned, Groenhoff effectively demonstrating the aerobatic capabilities of the Delta I and even spinning the aircraft! But once again the assembled officials were unimpressed, and when a certificate of airworthiness was applied for, Lippisch and his team received a long list of objections to the granting of the certificate, and the demand that a tailplane be fitted!

During the following winter, Groenhoff was seriously injured in a car accident in which his wife lost her life, and soon afterwards he attempted unsuccessfully to commit suicide. He never fully recovered from the tragedy and was to lose his life in a Fafnir sailplane during the Rhön Glider Competition of 1932—an enormous loss to German flying. Prior to this sad event, however, Lippisch received an order for a new machine, the Delta III, which had to be built at the Focke-Wulf plant in Bremen, and, simultaneously, Gerhard Fieseler of the Fieseler Works, a well-known aerobatic pilot, began work in collaboration with Lippisch on a twin-engined Delta which was known both as the Wespe (Wasp) and Delta IV. This type was a tandem two-seater with a small foreplane, and one engine drove a pusher airscrew while the other drove an orthodox tractor airscrew. Breaking his agreement with Lippisch, Fieseler flew the Delta IV and crashed during the landing approach. Fieseler promptly lost interest in the aircraft and, after repairs, flight testing was taken over by Groenhoff. However, the characteristics of the Delta IV were extremely poor, and Groenhoff had only completed half the test programme when he lost his life.

In the meantime, Lippisch had been endeavouring to obtain an order for the design and construction of

an all-wing bomber for the Aviation Department of the
Army Weapons' Establishment, the predecessor of
the Luftwaffe, but his proposals received the reply that the
low-wing arrangement was *unsuited* for military aircraft!
Lippisch's team moved to Darmstadt-Griesheim in 1933,
and following damage suffered during a taxiing accident,
the Delta III was rebuilt and fitted with a tractor airscrew.
The Delta IV was taken over from Fieseler, and the
rear engine with its pusher airscrew removed. The flight
test programme had been taken over by a pilot named
Wiegmeier, but after a few trials in its modified form
and with the foreplane removed, the Delta IV crashed.
At this time, the Delta III was being tested at Rechlin,
but the official test report was unfavourable. However,
Colonel (later General) Ritter von Greim decided to fly
the aircraft to see for himself if the official criticisms
were justified. His opinions were directly opposed to
the official view, but Wiegmeier, who had flown the
Delta III to Halle for a demonstration, crashed during
a take-off, and this disaster, coming within fourteen
days of the crash of the Delta IV, appeared to be the
death blow to Lippisch's hopes and aspirations.

A special commission was set up by the Air Ministry and the German Experimental Establishment for
Aviation to investigate the crashes, passing a resolution
forbidding the further development of such aircraft
which, it claimed, had neither practical value nor development potential. However, Doctor Walter Georgii, the
director of the German Research Institute for Sail-
planes (Deutsche Forschungsanstalt für Segelflug, or
DFS), came to Lippisch's aid by not only forcing the
commission to withdraw its ruling but also raising support for the reconstruction of the Delta IV which now
became the DFS 9 Delta IVb. The wing planform was
drastically modified and the small vertical surfaces at
the wingtips were supplanted by wingtips with marked
anhedral. Flight testing was taken over by Heini Dittmar
and, powered by a 75 h.p. Pobjoy engine driving a
tractor airscrew, the Delta IVb passed its full acceptance tests as a two-seat sporting aircraft.

In 1937, Doctor Lorenz, the assistant to Doctor A.

Baeumker, Chief of the Air Ministry's Research Department, ordered the construction of a second DFS 39. This was to feature a lengthened fuselage suitable to accommodate a "special power plant". At this time all rocket development was so secret that those engaged on it said jocularly that all documents should be stamped "To be burned before reading!" Lippisch's only comment when he realized that the special power plant was a liquid rocket was:—"My God!" The Ernst Heinkel plant had already been awarded a development contract for a rocket-propelled research aircraft, the He 176, and such was the secrecy that surrounded all such developments at this time that all design work on "Project X", as the rocket-driven DFS 39 was known, was undertaken in a specially constructed room. As the DFS did not have suitable facilities for the construction of the fuselage, it was decided that this should be built by Heinkel in the same section that was producing the He 176.

Like the He 176, the DFS 39 was to have a rocket motor evolved by Hellmuth Walter of Kiel whose work in this field had begun with a contract from the German Aviation Research Establishment for a small, well-calibrated rocket for making tests on the dynamic characteristics in roll of several aircraft. The rocket was to be fired on one wingtip and the time history of the roll displacement duly recorded. The thrust of this device was to be known exactly in order to attain accurate results. After unsuccessfully testing solid fuel rockets, the Research Establishment had turned to Walter whose main effort at that time was directed toward the use of hydrogen-peroxide and potassium-manganate for an underwater propulsion system for the German Navy. The rocket eventually produced by Walter had a thrust of ninety pounds, and was also used as a means of boosting the climb rate of light aircraft in a series of trials. The success of these tests resulted in the idea of using such devices for assisting the take-off of heavily-laden bombers, and around the same time, the first idea of a rocket-propelled interceptor began to mature. The immediate result was the contract for the He 176.

The He 176 featured diminutive wings, and after protracted tests in the Research Establishment's wind tunnel and innumerable modifications, it was found that the wing area was inadequate—the aircraft would not leave the ground! Initial trials were a fiasco, and it was not until entirely new wings of larger area were built and fitted to the aircraft that the He 176 eventually staggered off the ground, the initial flight being made on June 20th, 1939, and lasting fifty seconds! At this stage, historical facts become somewhat confused and contradictory. Professor Heinkel subsequently claimed that development of the He 176 fell victim of the short-sightedness of the Air Ministry, whereas Professor Lippisch has stated that the take-off of the He 176 proved extremely difficult, that no more than 215 m.p.h. was attained, and that the development potential of the aircraft was strictly limited. The Development Department of the Air Ministry was certainly disenchanted with the rocket insofar as its application to interceptor fighters was concerned!

In parallel with Project X, Lippisch was developing the DFS 40 and the DFS 194, both of which were intended for a single airscrew. Initially, the basic concept of these aircraft followed that of the DFS 39, but free flight model tests and extensive wind tunnel investigations revealed that directional stability and yaw-roll characteristics would be considerably improved with a swept wing without dihedral and a central fin-and-rudder assembly in place of the endplate surfaces. The aerodynamic performance obtained in large-scale wind tunnel tests made after these changes had been introduced proved to be exceptionally good, but by this time the political situation insofar as Lippisch was concerned was becoming increasingly difficult, and he decided, therefore, to leave Darmstadt and join the aircraft industry. Again, work at the DFS was continually harassed by security restrictions and other problems, and on January 2, 1939, Lippisch and twelve of his co-workers, including Hubert (aerodynamics), Sielaff (statics), Rentel (structures), Elias (workshops), Kropp (sheet metalwork), Armbrust, Görner, Brecht, Hartmann and, of course, the test pilot, Heini Dittmar, transferred to the Messerschmitt A.G. at Augsburg, forming Section 'L'.

The primary task of Section 'L' was the development of an operational rocket-powered interceptor, interest in which had reawakened in the meantime. The transition from work in a research institute to work in the aircraft industry brought the project into the orbit of the Aircraft Development Department of the Luftwaffe, and although the outbreak of war held up work temporarily, Section 'L' soon got down to the modification of the DFS 194 airframe for rocket power. The DFS 194 was transferred to Peenemünde from Augsburg early in 1940, and a Walter rocket motor of 1,650 lb. thrust was installed. This was of the so-called "cold" type, using T-stoff (eighty per cent hydrogen peroxide plus oxyquinoline or phosphate as a stabiliser) and Z-stoff (an aqueous solution of calcium permanganate). Flight trials were relatively successful, although, as was to have been expected, a number of problems were encountered. Nevertheless, although the airframe was not built for high speeds, Heini Dittmar attained 341.8 m.p.h. in the DFS 194.

The success of the DFS 194 brought about increased interest in the interceptor project which had been allocated the designation Me 163 and which had languished at Augsburg for many months with one of the lowest priority grades. The first of two prototype airframes was completed in the winter of 1940–41, and in the early Spring, Dittmar made the first gliding flights in the Me 163 V1* from Lechfeld. The aircraft was then towed to Augsburg by a Bf 110. However, coming in to land, Dittmar could not get the aircraft down, even on the large airfield at Augsburg. Only his skill as a pilot saved the aircraft—and his own life! Seeing that he was going to overshoot, Dittmar banked the prototype and glided through the narrow gap be-

---

*V1 indicating the first Versuch or Experimental model.

tween two hangars, touching down far beyond the airfield buildings.

Further test flights from Augsburg followed, all being towed starts. The first trials revealed an almost unbelievable gliding angle of 1:20! This was achieved despite the low aspect ratio of 1:44. The drag coefficient and small lift coefficients were 0.011. During high-speed gliding, Dittmar experienced dangerous rudder flutter at 225 m.p.h. and aileron flutter at 325 m.p.h. The flutter was the result of incorrect balancing and, once rectified, the flying characteristics of the aircraft were, in general, extraordinarily good. During one gliding flight, General Ernst Udet arrived at the airfield. Dittmar was flying at about sixteen thousand feet after casting off from his towplane and was about to begin his scheduled high-speed programme.

Udet joined Lippisch outside the hangars, pointed to the aircraft wheeling above, and said: "What's that, Lippisch?"

"The Me 163," replied Lippisch.

At that moment Dittmar put the aircraft into a steep dive and flashed past at substantially more than four hundred miles per hour, and then pulled up steeply.

"What kind of engine has it?" enquired Udet.

"None!" replied Lippisch, and laughed.

Once again Dittmar flashed down from above, soared several times around the field to use up his excess speed, and then came in to land.

"No engine! Impossible!" grunted Udet. With that, he ran across the field to the aircraft which had now come to a standstill. He examined the machine, and muttered: "It's true—there's no engine!"

Udet was so impressed by this performance that, after the project was fully explained to him, he promised his whole-hearted support, and promptly assisted in acquiring a higher priority grade for the Me 163, watching its subsequent development with keen interest until his suicide.

In the summer of 1941, the Me 163 V1 was sent to Peenemünde for powered tests, these taking place between July and October. Lippisch had now made a number of calculations which indicated that the aircraft could reach a maximum speed of 621 m.p.h. (1,000 km/h) with 880 lb. thrust at an altitude of 13,120 feet. During the first powered tests Dittmar had easily exceeded the existing world air speed record, and shortly afterwards speeds of 500 m.p.h. and 550 m.p.h. had been attained. A higher speed was achieved with each successive flight, these speeds being registered on the ground by six Ascania kinotheodolites, and on one flight, during which a speed of 571.78 m.p.h. was recorded, Dittmar experienced violent rudder flutter and lost control temporarily, although he succeeded in landing the aircraft in one piece.

The problem of attaining higher speeds centred on the quantity of fuel that the aircraft carried, this setting a limitation on the maximum speed reached before all fuel was exhausted of about 570 m.p.h. Dittmar then conceived the idea of conserving fuel by means of a tow to the altitude at which the speed runs were normally made. Accordingly, on October 2, 1941, the Me 163 V1 was towed to an altitude of thirteen thousand feet at which Dittmar cast off the towing cable and fired the rocket. A level speed of 623.85 m.p.h. was attained, this being the equivalent of Mach. 0.84, and then compressibility effects were experienced, the aircraft losing its stability. This flight would undoubtedly have caused an international sensation had it then been possible to reveal the facts to the world. They were, of course, buried beneath a thick cloak of secrecy. Dittmar's own comments made long after this remarkable flight were as follows:

"My speedometer soon read 910 km/hr and kept on climbing, soon topping the 1,000 km/hr mark. Then the needle began to waver, there was sudden vibration in the elevons and the next moment the aircraft went into an uncontrollable dive, causing strong negative acceleration. I immediately cut the rocket and, for a few moments, thought that I had really had it at last! Then, just as suddenly, the controls reacted again, and I eased the aircraft out of its dive. The so-called Mach phenomenon that I had just experienced was the first

knock on the door of the sound barrier which my
aircraft had not been built to penetrate."

The flight test measurements were evaluated during the same evening, and the results immediately forwarded to Berlin. However, most of the officials of the
Air Ministry simply did not want to believe the figures,
and Dr. Göthert from the Experimental Establishment
hurriedly arrived at Augsburg to check the figures for
himself. He was not in the least happy about the whole
business—his wind tunnel could only measure speeds
up to Mach 0.8 whereas the Me 163 had already flown
at Mach 0.84! Unlike the Air Ministry officials, Ernst
Udet was virtually bursting with eagerness and demand-
ing that weapons be fitted to the Me 163 as it was, there
and then!

Lippisch eventually succeeded in persuading Udet
that the existing rocket aircraft was no operational machine in any shape or form, and set about the redesign
of the Me 163 to take increased fuel, armament and
other operational equipment. Dittmar, in the meantime,
was awarded the highest decoration in the field of
powered flight, The Lilienthal Award for Aeronautical
Research. The new version, the Me 163B, was to receive a new Walter rocket motor with controllable thrust,
and construction of the prototype, the Me 163 V3,
began on December 1, 1941. This aircraft was ready
for test flying in April 1942, but the Walter rocket
motor was not ready for installation. Three successive
running tests had proved unsuccessful and, eventually,
Hellmuth Walter had to call in Doctor Schmitt who
succeeded in developing the new "hot" rocket to a state
where, although still far from reliable, it could be used
for flight trials.

While awaiting delivery of the rocket motor, gliding trials were conducted with the Me 163 V3, and
according to the reports of several test pilots, the handling characteristics were better than those of most
conventional aircraft. To prevent wingtip stall and to
simplify production, special low-drag fixed slots—so-
called C-slots—were fitted to the outboard wing panels,
and these proved highly effective. With crossed con-

trols the aircraft merely side-slipped. Heini Dittmar knew that he could not carry the sole responsibility for flight testing this radical aircraft much longer, and, with Udet's assistance, he succeeded in getting his old sailplane comrade, Rudolf Opitz, loaned to Messerschmitt to participate in the test programme.

Early in the test programme with the "hot" Me 163, Heini Dittmar was badly injured. In order to demonstrate an improved landing flap, he made a landing directly in front of a hangar where Lippisch and several of his technicians were assembled. Coming in to touch down, he glided into the windless space behind the hangar and stalled from an altitude of about twelve feet, hitting the concrete runway. As it happened, Dittmar was using a specially modified seat of his own design which did not permit any flexibility of movement. The result was severe damage to the spinal chord, and Dittmar was forced to languish in hospital for the next two years. Subsequently, Dr. Schneider made an extensive investigation into means of absorbing landing shocks, and the pilot's seat was fitted with emergency springing. Rudolf Opitz and Wolfgang Späte completed the remaining programme at Peenemünde, and then Späte was posted to Bad Zwischenahn to lead the newly-formed Test-Commando 16, the story of which is told in this book.

As time went by, Lippisch found it increasingly difficult to work with Professor Messerschmitt, early friction developing into open antagonism, and on May 1, 1943, he left Augsburg to take over an aeronautical research institute in Vienna. Development of the basic design continued and resulted in the Me 163C which attained the pre-production stage, and the Me 163D. At an early design state, the last-mentioned variant was handed over to Junkers at Dessau where a team headed by Professor Hertel undertook further redesign. For a brief period this development was redesignated Ju 248 but it eventually became known as the Me 263, the prototype being completed in August 1944.

In Vienna, Lippisch was working on the P 11, a high-speed twin-jet bomber of delta configuration, and the P 13 delta-wing interceptor powered by a ramjet. The P 13 was designed for supersonic flight from the outset, but neither the P 11 or P 13 were completed as, in June 1944, the entire plant in which they were being constructed was destroyed by bombing, and Lippisch lost thirty per cent of his personnel. It was then too late to transfer elsewhere, and Lippisch had to leave Vienna during Easter 1945 to avoid capture by the Russians.

Shortly after the war, Lippisch gave a lecture on delta wing aircraft in Paris–St. Germain before representatives of the American aircraft industry, the NACA and the USAF. After the lecture, a high official of the NACA said to Lippisch: "You know, Doctor, the Delta looks very simple but it is *too* unusual!" Nevertheless Lippisch had impressed von Karman who placed his influence behind the proposal to complete the glider model of the P 13 that had been under construction by the Darmstadt Group in Prien. In 1946, this model was tested in the NACA's full-scale wind tunnel, and after consulting Lippisch, Convair began delta development which led to the F-102A Delta Dagger and F-106A Delta Dart interceptors, and the B-58A Hustler bomber.

THE STUNNING NEW NOVEL BY THE
AUTHOR OF *MURDER AT THE RED OCTOBER*

MAY DAY IN MAGADAN

by Anthony Olcott

Critics called his first book, MURDER AT THE RED OCTOBER, "far superior to *Gorky Park*". Now Anthony Olcott returns with his newest triumph, MAY DAY IN MAGADAN. More than a highly suspenseful novel, this book is a vividly realized portrait of modern Russian life. From the dreams and frustrations of the common people, to the explosive power plays of Party bureaucrats—to the frightening drama of Ivan Duvakin, a man trapped by events beyond his control, a man running for his life. Once again, the reluctant hero of MURDER AT THE RED OCTOBER has been plunged into the vortex of a deadly conspiracy that reaches from the very top levels of Party command. His only ally is Galya, a woman doctor whose sensual charms mask a ferocious heart—a woman who may be his ultimate betrayer.

"A richly detailed gallery of Soviets ... a Russianness which is unrelenting, nearly palpable ... irresistible."
—*The Washington Post*

Don't miss MAY DAY IN MAGADAN, on sale June 15, 1984, wherever Bantam Books are sold—or use the handy coupon below for ordering:

THE BLISTERING NEW THRILLER BY
THE BESTSELLING AUTHOR OF
AN EXCHANGE OF EAGLES

THE
KREMLIN
CONTROL

OWEN SELA

With a single, cryptic clue to guide him, KGB officer Yuri
Raikin pierces the heart of a monstrous secret hidden for three
decades . . . A secret that explains a general's death and an
agent who should have died . . . A secret of conspiracy that
reaches from Moscow to Zurich to Washington . . . A secret
so explosive that it could topple the walls of the Kremlin—and
shatter world peace forever.

Read **The Kremlin Control,** a stunning novel of Russian intrigue
and treachery, on sale August 15, 1984, wherever Bantam
paperbacks are sold, or use the handy coupon below for
ordering:

Join the Allies on the Road to Victory
BANTAM WAR BOOKS

THE AVIATOR'S BOOKSHELF

THE CLASSICS OF FLYING

The books that aviators, test pilots, and astronauts feel tell the most about the skills that launched mankind on the adventure of flight. These books bridge man's amazing progress, from the Wright brothers to the first moonwalk.

☐ **THE WRIGHT BROTHERS by Fred C. Kelly** (23962-7 • $2.95)
Their inventive genius was enhanced by their ability to learn how to fly their machines.

☐ **THE FLYING NORTH by Jean Potter** (23946-5 • $2.95)
The Alaskan bush pilots flew in impossible weather, frequently landing on sandbars or improvised landing strips, flying the early planes in largely uninhabited and unexplored land.

☐ **THE SKY BEYOND by Sir Gordon Taylor** (23949-X • $2.95)
Transcontinental flight required new machines piloted by skilled navigators who could pinpoint tiny islands in the vast Pacific—before there were radio beacons and directional flying aids.

☐ **THE WORLD ALOFT by Guy Murchie** (23947-3 • $2.95)
The book recognized as *The Sea Round Us* for the vaster domain—the Air. Mr. Murchie, a flyer, draws from history, mythology and many sciences. The sky is an ocean, filled with currents and wildlife of its own. A tribute to, and a celebration of, the flyers' environment.

☐ **CARRYING THE FIRE by Michael Collins** (23948-1 • $3.50)
"The best written book yet by any of the astronauts."—*Time Magazine*. Collins, the Gemini 10 and Apollo 11 astronaut, gives us a picture of the joys of flight and the close-in details of the first manned moon landing.

☐ **THE LONELY SKY by William Bridgeman with Jacqueline Hazard** (23950-3 • $3.50)
The test pilot who flew the fastest and the highest. The excitement of going where no one has ever flown before by a pilot whose careful study and preparation was matched by his courage.

Read all of the books in THE AVIATOR'S BOOKSHELF

Prices and availability subject to change without notice

Buy them at your bookstore or use this handy coupon for ordering:

SPECIAL
MONEY SAVING
OFFER

Now you can have an up-to-date listing of Bantam's hundreds of titles plus take advantage of our unique and exciting bonus book offer. A special offer which gives you the opportunity to purchase a Bantam book for only 50¢. Here's how!

By ordering any five books at the regular price per order, you can also choose any other single book listed (up to a $4.95 value) for just 50¢. Some restrictions do apply, but for further details why not send for Bantam's listing of titles today!

Just send us your name and address plus 50¢ to defray the postage and handling costs.